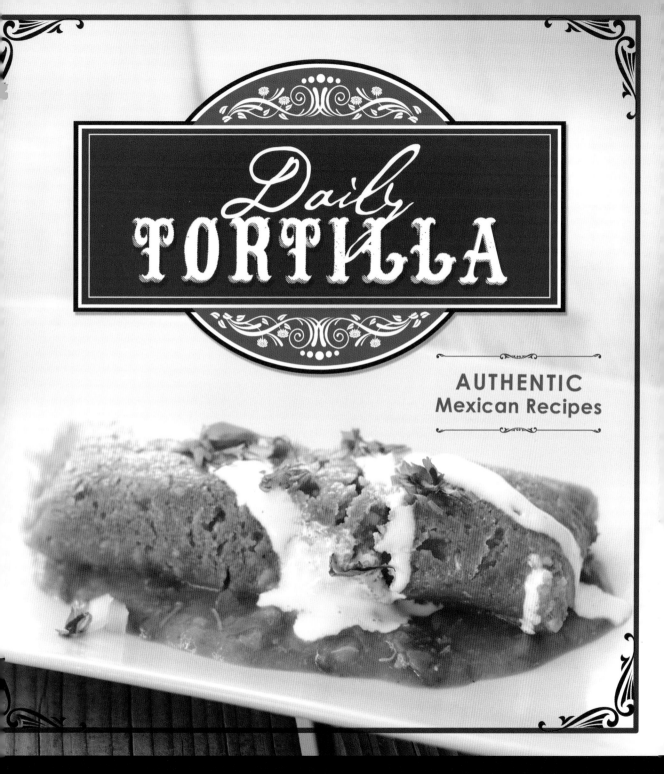

# Daily TORTILLA

## AUTHENTIC
## Mexican Recipes

# RICARDO JAMES

FRONT TABLE BOOKS | AN IMPRINT OF CEDAR FORT, INC. | SPRINGVILLE, UTAH

ISBN 13: 978-1-4621-1411-5

Published by Front Table Books, an imprint of Cedar Fort, Inc.
2373 W. 700 S., Springville, UT 84663
Distributed by Cedar Fort, Inc., www.cedarfort.com

Library of Congress Cataloging-in-Publication Data

James, Ricardo.
  Daily tortilla : authentic Mexican recipes / Ricardo James.
       pages cm
  Includes index.
  ISBN 978-1-4621-1411-5
  1.  Cooking, Mexican.  I. Title.
  TX716.M4J36 2014
  641.5972--dc23
                                  2014003775

Cover and page design by Erica Dixon
Cover design © 2014 by Lyle Mortimer
Edited by Casey J. Winters

Printed in the United States of America

10  9  8  7  6  5  4  3  2  1

For Esperanza "Pera" Herrera,
who shared her home, her kitchen, and her love.
I will miss you.

# CONTENTS

# ACKNOWLEDGMENTS

*I am both grateful and humbled to have the opportunity to share my version of authentic Mexican recipes with you. Each recipe reflects the personality of the cook, and the quality of the ingredients determines the outcome. Not seen, but surely tasted, is the love, effort, and passion that the cook infuses into each dish. The result can potentially alter your thinking, change your frame of mind, and affect your personal well-being.*

1 enabling and caring mother who entrusted her kitchen to me from a young age (Dorothy)

A handful of experienced native mentors willing to coach and share (Pera, Norma, and Mama Figueroa)

1 patient and loving wife who knows how to type (Judy)

5 honest and eager children who try everything I cook (Wesley, Tyler, Olivia, Brandon, and Andrew)

1 neighborhood full of taste testers

1 abundantly enthusiastic father who tells me every recipe is the best I've ever made (Chuck)

1 foodie friend eager to help publish these recipes (Ben)

1 talented photographer who somewhat refrained from eating the food before the pictures were taken (Greg)

1 brilliant son with an expert eye for photos (Andrew)

1 Mix all ingredients together and stew over a lifetime.

2 Infuse with passion for Mexican history, culture, and food.

3 Serve to family and friends topped with laughter and good times.

Makes for a happy cook.

ix

# INTRODUCTION

O ne hundred miles northwest of Mexico City lies Querétaro. Historically rich and very diverse, the once capital city is one of my favorite places on earth. I was a twenty-year-old missionary when I lived there, which meant I hardly ever cooked for myself. I relied on Mexican hospitality provided by friends of our cause, or I ate on the street. Either way I ate a lot of traditional Mexican food.

I practically lived in a cave on a hillside underneath a very old convent. On the corner in front of the church was a taco stand that was only open in the evenings. After a long day's work, I'd arrive tired and hungry. Ten tacos al pastor later, I would crash and dream in Spanish. It became a nightly ritual I still think about today.

Thirty yeas later and not much wiser, resistance proves futile if I spot a stand with tacos al pastor; however, now I can only eat two to three of the small double-tortilla pockets of tangy pork charred on a spit. These tacos are topped minimally with minced cilantro, white onion, and perhaps a dab of green salsa. Whoa! I'm getting ahead of myself. We'll get to plenty of that tangy goodness later in these pages. But first, what is authentic Mexican food?

When I was growing up, my mother, had four go-to Mexican recipes: pancake-style enchiladas, taco salad, sour cream chicken enchiladas, and tacos. I loved them—they helped inspire me to be a chef, and I cook them often for my family. However, none of them were truly authentic Mexican food. They were all southwestern cuisine, or what I refer to as Tex-Mex.

Several characteristics make a dish authentic. Foremost, Mexican food is fresh. South-of-the-border kitchens have small refrigerators, so food is purchased in the morning, cooked midday, and consumed in the late afternoon each and every day. Any leftovers are eaten that evening. I'm overgeneralizing a bit, but Mexicans usually don't have leftovers, and they go to the market every day. I now realize why my wife thinks I go to the super market much too often—because I do!

Second, authentic Mexican recipes normally include a delivery mechanism, or what I'll call a platform, such as the tortilla, tostada, or tamale. I believe platforms are included for several reasons. Mexican food is personal. It comes in small, individual packages so it can be eaten with your hands. Platforms are inexpensive, and they extend the food farther within a limited economy.

Third, authentic Mexican food consists of a limited number of ingredients utilized in many different combinations and cooking methods. Imagine a typical Mexican housewife. She can cook a different meal each day of the week merely by going to the corner tienda (store). The tienda might be a single room on the main floor of the house on the corner. It might only sell a limited number of ingredients (whereas a single aisle of my local supermarket offers a bigger selection). With these ingredients, she can make a diverse collection of recipes.

Last, a good friend asked me what would set my book apart from other Mexican cookbooks. My response was that I only included authentic recipes, cooked by everyday housewives, using fresh ingredients, with traditional methods. Traditional Mexican methods or techniques set the cuisine apart from French or American fare. Some of the most commonly used tools in a Mexican kitchen are a blender, pressure cooker, and metal strainer. In preparing this book, I found myself repeatedly using these tools in my recipes.

My goal with this book is to present simple, common recipes found in Mexican homes with exact technique so the reader can enjoy the pleasures of great Mexican food. As Americans, we tend to apply American techniques and twists to Mexican ingredients and flavors, and we end up with Tex-Mex. I will refrain from deviating from the traditional and leave the exploration to you.

# THE BASICS

**M**any foods around the world have certain characteristics that make them unique to outsiders but commonplace for residents. Take beans (frijoles), for example. As Americans, we think of beans as a side accompanied with rice, seldom presented any other way. Mexicans eat beans almost every day—not every meal, but almost, without question, every day. Beans are inexpensive and a common staple all over the world. Typically high in fiber, calcium, and iron, beans are also a great source of protein. Yes, they can be used as a side, but they can also be an ingredient or a topping. Eggs are the most common companion to beans in Mexico. Beans can even be used as the main and only event at the dinner table.

The basics in Mexican cooking are those foods that accompany every meal: salsas, guacamoles, moles, and frijoles. These aren't condiments that you take or leave like mustard or relish. Without the basics, Mexican food would not be complete. Condiments do exist—such as queso, crema, lettuce, cabbage, and, of course, chile peppers—but these basics are recipes themselves and are integral parts of larger dishes.

Presented here are my favorite basics found in Mexican cooking.

# SALSAS

There are as many salsas as there are chiles. Salsas consist of three components: bulk, heat, and spice. The main ingredient of a salsa is the bulk component. It carries the salsa. Typically jitomates (red tomatoes) or tomatillos (green tomatoes) take center stage as the main ingredient of most salsas; however, beans and corn can bulk up a salsa nicely.

The heat component of salsa comes from chile peppers. These come in many forms:

1. Dry powders, simply called chile, from chiles like árbol or chipotle, are most common.

2. Freshly chopped chile peppers such as jalapeños or serranos.

3. Chopped roasted peppers such as anaheims or poblanos.

4. Raw pureed peppers like the serrano.

5. Cooked pureed chilies such as guajillo or chipotle.

Hundreds of combinations exist.

The third component, spice, usually consists of salt, onions, garlic, fruit, or other ingredients that can enhance the final dish and give sweetness, texture, or crunch.

# PICO DE GALLO

## Mexican Salsa | Time: 10 minutes

*Pico de gallo, literally translated as "rooster beak salsa," is fresh salsa, meaning no component is cooked. Mexicans can't tell you why it is called pico de gallo, but they will tell you it's purely authentic because it presents the colors of the Mexican flag: red, green, and white.*

**3–4 tomatoes, diced and juices drained**

**1 serrano or jalapeño chile, minced**

**1 small white onion, diced**

**1 Tbsp. vinegar or lime juice**

**½ tsp. salt**

**Makes about 2 cups**

1   Mix all ingredients in a bowl.

2   Serve with everything!

8

# SALSA RANCHERA

## Ranch Salsa | Time: 25 minutes

*Outdoor taco stands, found on many Mexican street corners, commonly offer two or three salsas with which the buyer can either drizzle or smother their morsels of delight. I love the freshness of this salsa. It's great on tacos or with tortilla chips.*

**4 fresh garden tomatoes, whole**

**½ red bell pepper**

**4 garlic cloves, whole**

**1 Tbsp. vegetable oil**

**¼ white onion, minced and rinsed**

**2 Tbsp. cilantro, minced**

**1 tsp. salt**

**½–1 tsp. chile de árbol powder**

**Makes 4 cups**

1  Heat a gas grill to 400+ degrees. (For an indoor option use your oven broiler.)

2  Place tomatoes and bell pepper directly on the grill and char. It may take 10–15 minutes. They will be warmed through and the tomato skins will begin to fall off.

3  Quarter the tomatoes and place in a blender with the pepper.

4  Heat oil and fry the garlic whole until lightly brown. Add to the blender.

5  Add minced onion to the blender and pulse on low until tomatoes are broken completely but onions are the size of rice.

NOTE  *Be careful not to puree your salsa. The garlic and onions will overpower the delicateness of the tomatoes and the pepper if you overdo it.*

6  Pour salsa into a serving bowl and stir in the cilantro.

7  Add salt and chile powder a little at a time, tasting for heat and salt. Chill.

# SALSA DE CHILE ANCHO Y JITOMATE

## Roasted Ancho Chile and Tomato Salsa
## Time: 30 minutes

*This classic salsa is rustic in flavor. Traditionally it is made in a molcajete, the Mexican version of a mortar and pestle. If you don't have a molcajete, simply mash as you chop the vegetables.*

**2 ancho chiles**

**8 tomatoes, whole**

**1 small white onion, halved**

**2 cloves garlic**

**1 tsp. cayenne chile powder**

**1 tsp. salt**

**juice of 1 lime**

**1 tsp. dried oregano**

**¼ cup fresh cilantro, chopped**

**Makes approx. 6 cups**

1  On a gas grill (or in a broiler set to 500 degrees), roast the chiles, tomatoes, onion halves, and garlic cloves for 8–10 minutes. Turn once. The tomato skins will begin to fall off.

2  Enclose chiles in a paper grocery bag. This will allow the chiles to sweat, making it easier to peel the skins off. Set other vegetables aside to cool.

3  After 10 minutes, remove the chiles from the bag and peel off the tough skins. Rinse in a trickle of water to remove seeds. Remove the stems.

4  Remove the tomato skins. Place chiles, tomatoes, onions, garlic, and cayenne pepper in a molcajete and crush into a salsa.

5  Add salt, lime juice, oregano, and cilantro. Crush the oregano as you add it to the salsa. This will help bring out more of those aromatic flavors.

6  Chill and serve.

12

Ricardo James

# SALSA VERDE CON AGUACATE

## Roasted Green Salsa with Avocado
Time: 20 minutes

*A superb change of pace from the traditional pico de gallo (page 8). When it comes to salsa that can enhance any dish, I would have to elect this salsa verde. It has a tangy punch, but the avocados give it a creamy texture. It is great on sopes, tacos, and even chips.*

1 Tbsp. olive oil

6–8 tomatillos, halved

1 small white onion, sliced

1–2 serrano chiles, halved lengthwise

2 garlic cloves, mashed

1½ cups water

²/₃ cup cilantro, chopped

¾ cup water

1–1½ tsp. salt

1 avocado, pitted and diced

Makes about 4 cups

**The preparation can be done several ways:**

**1A**  Rub tomatillos, onion, chiles, and garlic with olive oil and place on a sheet pan. Roast under the broiler for 5–8 minutes, until charred.

**OR**

**1B**  Heat a griddle (comal) until very hot and roast the tomatillos, onion, chiles, and garlic on the griddle until charred.

**OR**

**1C**  Boil the tomatillos, onion, chiles, and garlic in 1½ cups water in a small sauté pan until medium tender.

**OR**

**1D**  Rub tomatillos, onion, chiles, and garlic with olive oil and char over hot gas or charcoal grill.

Ricardo James

**2** After cooking the vegetables, place them in a blender or food processor with cilantro and ¾ cup water. Pulse on low until slightly chunky.

**3** Taste and season with salt. Add half of the avocado and pulse for 3–4 seconds.

**4** Pour salsa into a bowl and add the remaining diced avocado. Serve warm or cold.

# SALSA DE TOMATILLO

## Fresh Green Salsa | Time: 10 minutes

*In this salsa, nothing is cooked. The fresher your ingredients the better. This is great on fish; try pairing it with fish taquitos (page 94).*

**4–5 large tomatillos; husked, cleaned, and chopped**

**1 small white onion, diced, divided**

**1–2 serrano chiles, minced**

**¾ cup cilantro, chopped**

**1 tsp. salt**

**Makes 2 cups**

1. In a blender, place the tomatillos, half of the onion, the chiles, the cilantro, and the salt.

2. Carefully pulse until desired consistency—should be chunky

3. Add remaining onions. Chill and serve.

17

# GUACAMOLE

## Time: 10 minutes

*The avocado is the magical fruit. It is versatile in so many ways: used in dips, side dishes, main dishes, soups, appetizers, salads, sandwiches, and even desserts. From this magical fruit comes guacamole.*

*If you could choose one dish (which you can't) that is quintessential of Mexican cooking, it might be guacamole. It is the accompaniment of all accompaniments. Guacamole transforms the avocado from its neutral, bland-flavor state to a garlicky, salty, spicy goodness that is the definition of a great dip.*

*Here I present a simple classic recipe for guacamole. There are only 5 ingredients. Including additional ingredients will give your guacamole a uniqueness that will make it memorable, and you can lean the flavor toward the food it will accompany. For example, including bacon bits adds a smoky depth of flavor that pairs well with meat, potato, and cheese dishes. Adding a fruit such as raspberries or mangoes is great for hot summer days, giving the guacamole a lightly sweet taste. Adding roasted peppers will pair well with fish or is great for dips. If done right, guacamole is the most flavorful Mexican accompaniment. This recipe may surprise you in how simple it is to make.*

**2–3 ripe avocados (keep 1 seed aside)**

**3 cloves garlic (1 for every avocado)**

**¼ cup fresh cilantro, chopped**

**juice of 1 lime**

**1 tsp. salt**

**Makes 2–3 cups**

1   Cut the avocados in half lengthwise.

2   Cut a grid in the flesh but not through the skin.

3   Scoop the flesh into a bowl and mash with a fork.

4   Push the garlic through a press and add it to the bowl.

5   Add the cilantro and gently mix, leaving chunks.

6   Add lime juice and salt to taste.

**NOTE**   *Guacamole needs more salt than most other salsas. Keep the remaining seed in the prepared guacamole to slow the undesired browning process.*

## VARIATIONS COULD INCLUDE

Shrimp, raspberries, mango (or any other kind of fruit), squeezed lime, or bacon bits.

· · · · · · · · · · · · · · · **How to Pick a Ripe Avocado** · · · · · · · · · · · · · ·

Trying to find avocados that are just right to make guacamole can be tricky. Here are some tips:

- When you hold an avocado in your hand and press with your thumb—it should give way ever so slightly.

- If it does not give at all, it is too green and can't be used yet. If it feels mushy or gives way too easily, it is overripe and should not be used.

- Avoid avocados with skin that is uneven or sunken in spots.

# MOLE POBLANO O MOLE ROJO

Red Mole
Time: 90 minutes

*I remember the first time I had mole poblano. I was a foreign exchange student living in Hermosillo, Mexico, and my professor had been invited to a friend's home to have dinner. He invited me along but warned me that we were going to have mole poblano, which wasn't one of his favorite foods. I went along and thought the mole was just okay. Over the years I have learned to love the rich, dark sauce with a hint of chocolate served with chicken. I agree that it is an acquired taste, but it is one of those dishes that is prepared only for special occasions, such as having friends over for dinner. It is a traditional meal with turkey for Christmas or with chicken for a birthday dinner. I think it is held in such high esteem because it takes so long to prepare.*

*Tradition has it that Catholic nuns, upon learning that the archbishop was coming for a visit, went into a panic because they had nothing special to serve him. The nuns started praying desperately, and an angel came to inspire them. They began chopping and grinding and roasting, mixing different types of chiles together with spices, day-old bread, nuts, a little chocolate, and approximately twenty other ingredients. This concoction boiled for hours and was reduced to the thick, sweet, rich, and fragrant mole sauce we know today. They killed the only meat source they had, an old turkey, and the strange sauce was poured over it. The archbishop was more than happy with his banquet, and the nuns saved face. Little did they know they were creating what would become the Mexican national dish for holidays and feasts, or that today, millions of people worldwide have at least heard of mole poblano. This recipe makes two quarts and keeps well in the fridge or freezer.*

Ricardo James

3 Tbsp. vegetable oil

4 dried pasilla chiles, stems and seeds removed, cut into small pieces

8 dried New Mexican chiles, stems and seeds removed, cut into small pieces

1 medium onion, chopped

2 cloves garlic, chopped

2 Tbsp. sesame seeds

½ cup almonds

1 piece dried rustic bread, broken into small pieces

½ cup raisins

2 medium tomatoes, chopped, divided

4 cups chicken broth, divided

½ banana

½ cup creamy peanut butter

1 cup sugar

1 tsp. ground cloves

1 tsp. ground cinnamon

1 tsp. round coriander

1 tsp. chipotle chile powder

2 tsp. salt

1 round Mexican chocolate (Abuelita brand)

Makes approx. 2 quarts

1  In a large frying pan, heat 1 tablespoon of oil (add more as necessary). Fry each of the following items one at a time until golden and remove to a large bowl: chiles, onion, garlic, sesame seeds, almonds, bread, and raisins.

2  Put half of the fried ingredients into a blender with half of the tomatoes.

3  Add 2 cups of chicken broth to the blender and puree until very smooth.

4  Pour contents of blender into a large bowl and set aside.

5  Put remaining fried ingredients into the blender with the remaining tomatoes.

6  Add banana, peanut butter, sugar, remaining broth, spices, and salt.

7  Heat the chocolate round in the microwave for 30–45 seconds and add to the blender. Puree until very smooth.

8  Push all pureed ingredients through a strainer. Discard the dregs.

9  In a large pot, heat the mole through. Simmer on very low for 30–40 minutes. Stir constantly to avoid burning.

10  Taste and add salt or sugar if needed.

11  Add more broth if the mole is too thick.

NOTE  *Mole is traditionally served with roasted chicken, turkey, or tamales and rice. It can also be used as a condiment on grilled shrimp with lime juice instead of cocktail sauce.*

21

# ENCHILADA SAUCE

Time: 10 minutes

*Making your own enchilada sauce can be an eye-opening experience. You'll see how easy it is, and you might never again rip open a package of dried enchilada mix from the supermarket. This recipe yields about two quarts of sauce and can be kept in the fridge for a month. I use it on huevos rancheros (page 80) and chilaquiles (page 82).*

**10–15 dried chiles**
  **(I like a mixture of ancho chiles with one of the following: guajillo, New Mexico, or California. You can always add a few hotter chiles if you need a little more heat.)**

**water**

**3 garlic cloves, roughly chopped**

**1 can tomato sauce**

**2 tsp. salt**

**4 Tbsp. shortening or lard**

**⅓ cup flour**


**Makes 2 quarts**

1 Preheat your oven to 400 degrees. Clean the chiles. Using kitchen shears, cut the stems off and cut a slit down the side to remove all veins and seeds from each chile. Place them on a baking sheet, and roast them for 3½–4 minutes. Keep a watchful eye—when they start to turn dark and smoke, they are done. If you overcook the chiles, you'll run everyone out of the house, so be careful.

2 While the chiles roast, bring 5–6 cups of water to a boil in a large pot.

3 Remove the chiles from the baking sheet and place them directly in the boiling water. Lower the heat and simmer the chiles uncovered for 10 minutes, until they become limp and tender.

4 Drain the liquid and transfer the chiles to a blender. Add about 3 cups of water and the garlic cloves, tomato sauce, and salt. Puree on high until very smooth.

5 Push the sauce through a strainer. This removes any seeds and the large pieces of chile.

**NOTE** *I use a wooden spoon with my metal strainer to push the chile sauce through.*

22

**6** In a large heavy pot or dutch oven, heat the shortening or lard on medium heat. Add the flour and make a rue by stirring until golden. It should take a minute or two.

**7** Remove the pot from the heat. Add the sauce carefully, stirring constantly.

**8** Return the pot to the heat and add an additional 2 cups of water. Simmer on medium, stirring constantly, for about 5 minutes. The sauce should thicken and coat the back of a spoon.

**9** Cool and refrigerate in glass jars until needed. (Don't use plastic storage containers—they will stain.)

# FRIJOLES DE OLLA

Pot Beans (the essential side dish)
Time: 10 minutes and 45-minute cook time

*Pot beans are, along with rice, the overly typical side dish of Mexican cuisine. But beans made the traditional way are nothing like canned beans. Pot beans are the first step to making refried beans, or frijoles refritos. When made correctly, pot beans are an earthy comfort food that completes any Mexican meal. They can be topped with any kind of salsa or cheese to take on a variety of flavors.*

*Note: I used a pressure cooker to cook the beans. This trims off cooking time without sacrificing flavor. If you don't have a pressure cooker, use a large pot and lengthen the simmering time to 3 hours, or until the beans are tender.*

**1 lb. dried pinto beans**

**2 slices bacon,
or 2 tablespoons lard**

**2 cloves garlic, slightly
mashed**

**½ medium white onion,
sliced**

**2–3 tsp. salt**

**1 sprig epazote (found in
your local latin market), or
cilantro**

**Makes 6 cups beans
in broth**

1 Clean the beans: Spread them on your counter space. Pick out any dirt clods or discolored beans. Place the good beans in a colander and wash with warm water—you will be surprised at the amount of dirt that comes off.

2 Place the beans in a pressure cooker and cover with 1 inch of water above the beans. Nothing else should be added at this point. Do not put on the lid.

3 Bring the beans to a rolling boil for 5 minutes. Let stand in the hot water for 10 more minutes.

4 Pour the beans back into the colander and rinse well with warm water.

5 Rinse the pressure cooker and place the beans back in and cover with 2 inches of water above the beans. Add the bacon (or lard), smashed garlic, sliced onion, salt, and epazote sprig (or cilantro).

**6** Seal the pressure cooker and cook on high until it starts to steam. Lower the heat and pressure for 30 minutes. The total time should take just less than 1 hour. While the beans pressure cook, you can usually complete the rest of the meal.

**7** After the pressure time is up, turn off the heat and let the pot sit until you are ready to serve dinner. Follow your cooker's instructions to cool it down.

**8** Remove the bacon, garlic, epazote and onion from the pot if you want. Taste for salt and add more if necessary.

The beans can be served with a rich amount of broth, more like a soup, or in a small bowl so the broth doesn't run all over your plate. You can eat them plain or topped with pico de gallo, salsa verde, or even a mole. I love them with any type of cheese or sour cream.

**NOTE** *Mexicans will make a big pot using 2 pounds of beans and use it at each meal for a couple of days. Some rendition of beans is eaten at every meal. When you get to the bottom of the pot, it's time to make refried beans (see page 26).*

# FRIJOLES REFRITOS

## Refried Beans | Time: 15 minutes

*Refried beans, to me, have always had the connotation of being leftovers, but they don't have to be. I know many a señora that will make pot beans (see page 24) with the only intention to make them into frijoles refritos. Even if I have to resort to using canned beans, I still follow this recipe so they taste a little bit more authentic.*

**2–3 strips good bacon, chopped small**

**3 cups frijoles de olla (page 24)**

**½ cup of your favorite cheese (I prefer queso fresco)**

**Makes 4–6 servings**

1 In a large heavy frying pan or dutch oven, cook the bacon until crispy.

2 Remove from the heat and add the beans.

3 Using a potato masher, mash most of the beans while still warm. (The bottom of a plastic drinking glass works great as well.)

4 Stir in the cheese and heat through.

5 Serve with everything!

**NOTE** *For frijoles refritos enchilados, add 1 cup enchilada sauce (page 22) at the end.*

# FRIJOLES CON CARNE

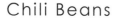

Chili Beans
Time: 10 minutes and 45-minute cook time

*This is a great diversion from the simple frijoles de olla (page 24). By adding the chorizo, the end result is a pot of beans with an attitude. It can be used as an entire meal.*

*Note: Chorizo originally came from Spain, but Mexico has its own spin on the freshly made pork sausage. Unlike the European version, Mexican chorizo needs to be cooked before consuming. It is a great accompaniment to potatoes or eggs, or with cheese in queso fundido (page 60). In this recipe, the chorizo is completely dissolved into the broth. It adds subtle depth of flavor that can't be reached by other means.*

**1 lb. dried pinto beans**

**1 lb. chorizo, casings removed, chopped**

**2 cloves garlic, minced**

**½ medium white onion, diced**

**1 tsp. salt**

**1 sprig cilantro**

**Serves 6 as a meal**

**Serves 8 as a side dish**

1  Clean the beans: Spread them on your counter space. Pick out any dirt clods or discolored beans. Place the good beans in a colander and wash with warm water.

2  Place the beans in a pressure cooker and cover with 1 inch of water above the beans. Nothing else should be added at this point. Do not put on the lid.

3  Bring the beans to a rolling boil for 5 minutes. Let stand in the hot water for 10 more minutes.

4  Pour the beans back into the colander and rinse well with warm water.

5  Rinse the pressure cooker and place the beans back in and cover with 2 inches of water above the beans. Add the chorizo, garlic, onion, salt, and cilantro.

**6** Seal the pressure cooker and cook on high until it starts to steam. Lower the heat, and pressure for 30 minutes.

**7** After the pressure time is up, turn off the heat and let the pot sit until you are ready to serve dinner. Follow your cooker's instructions to cool it down.

**8** Taste for salt and add more if necessary.

# ARROZ A LA MEXICANA

## Mexican Rice | Time: 45 minutes

*A companion to beans, rice plays an important role in completing a Mexican meal. This recipe is a breeze to make.*

6 Tbsp. vegetable oil, divided

½ medium white onion

2 cloves garlic, mashed but whole

1 serrano chile

2 cups chopped tomatoes

4 cups chicken broth

2 cups rice

1 chicken bouillon cube

Serves 8

1  In 3 tablespoons of the oil, sauté the onion, garlic, and chile until tender.

2  Transfer the cooked vegetables to a blender. Add the tomatoes and broth, and puree until smooth.

3  Heat the remaining 3 tablespoons of oil in a large pan. Add the rice and cook until puffy and white, about 3 minutes. Stir continually.

4  Remove from the heat. Add the puree and bouillon cube.

5  Cover and simmer on very low for 20 minutes, or until all the liquid has evaporated. Keep warm.

6  Fluff with a fork and serve.

NOTE  *Different as it may seem, Mexicans love to eat bananas with their rice, as shown in the photo.*

# POLLO ROSTIZADO

## Roasted Chicken
## Time: 10 minutes and 45-minute cook time

*This simple cooking technique can be used to prepare any chicken dish calling for roasted chicken. I use it for tinga, enchiladas, tamales, tacos, and more.*

**4 chicken breasts, skin on, bone in**

**1 Tbsp. salt**

**Makes 4 cups**

1  Heat oven to 400 degrees.

2  Place chicken on a baking sheet. Generously sprinkle with salt, and bake 45 minutes.

3  When juices run clear, chicken is done. Remove from oven to cool.

4  Remove skin, and debone.

5  Store in airtight container in refrigerator for up to 2 days. Keep whole until used—this keeps the chicken moist.

# ARROZ BLANCO

## Rice with Chicken Broth | Time: 25 minutes

3 Tbsp. vegetable oil

½ medium white onion, sliced

2 cloves garlic, mashed but whole

2 cups rice

6 cups chicken broth

2–3 tsp. salt

Serves 8

1 Heat the oil in a dutch oven.

2 Add the sliced onion and garlic, and fry until golden brown.

3 Remove the onion and garlic and discard.

4 Add the rice and cook until puffy and white, about 3 minutes. Stir continually.

5 Add broth and salt. Cover and simmer on low, stirring occasionally, for 15 minutes, or until all the liquid has evaporated. Keep warm.

6 Fluff with a fork.

NOTE For garlic rice, add 2 more cloves of minced garlic with the broth. Other additional flavors you might consider: thyme, parsley, and/or bay leaf. Time for garlic rice: 30 minutes.

Ricardo James

# CREMA MEXICANA

## Mexican Cream | Time: 5 minutes

*To add richness to a dish or mellow the spice, drizzle crema Mexicana on just about anything.*

½ **cup cream or half-and-half**

2 **cups sour cream**

**Makes 2½ cups**

**1**  Whisk together ingredients.

**NOTE**  *I like to keep my Crema Mexicana in a squeezable plastic bottle, which I can store in the refrigerator. It makes it easy to finish plating a dish.*

# CEBOLLAS EN VINAGRE

## Pickled Onions
## Time: 10 minutes and 15-minute marinate time

*These tangy strings of delight are fantastic topped on tacos, stuffed in gorditas, or piled on tortas. They are quick and easy to make, and they will become one of your favorite toppings.*

**1 red or white onion, sliced super thin**

**1 cup white vinegar**

**1 jalapeño chile, sliced thin (optional)**

**1 Tbsp. sugar (optional)**

**Makes 1 cup**

1. Place all ingredients in a glass bowl. Mix to combine.

2. Let marinate for at least 15 minutes. This can be prepared a day ahead.

3. Drain before serving.

# CHIMICHURRI DE AJO Y CHILE

## Garlic and Red Chile Salsa | Time: 45 minutes

*This recipe breaks the rule and does not include a bulk ingredient such as tomatoes or tomatillos. It has a pungent, tangy flavor. Use it when you need a lot of flavor but don't have a lot of space.*

**4 guajillo chiles, dried**

**hot water**

**2 garlic cloves, chopped**

**3 Tbsp. olive oil**

**¼ tsp. dried oregano**

**¼ tsp. salt**

Makes ½ cup

1. Using kitchen shears, cut off the ends of each chile. Cut down one side of each chile, and remove veins and seeds. Cut into very small pieces.

2. Soak chiles in small bowl of hot water for 30 minutes to rehydrate.

3. Drain the chile and transfer to a blender.

4. Add garlic, oil, oregano, and salt. Puree until nearly smooth.

5. Transfer to a small bowl and serve.

Ricardo James

# CHIMICHURRI VERDE

## Garlic and Green Chile Salsa
## Time: 45 minutes

*This tangy condiment is great on fish and tacos al pastor (page 92). This salsa is made with two versions of the same chile. (The poblano chile is sometimes referred to as an ancho chile.) The fresh chile provides bulk while the dried chile adds more spice.*

**1 dried poblano chile, whole**

**1 fresh poblano chile; peeled, cleaned, and chopped**

**1 large tomatillo, chopped**

**1 garlic clove, chopped**

**3 Tbsp. olive oil**

**¼ tsp. salt**

**Makes ½ cup**

1  Using kitchen shears, cut off ends of the dried chile. Cut down one side of the chile, and remove veins and seeds. Cut into very small pieces.

2  Soak chile in small bowl of water for 30 minutes to rehydrate.

3  Drain the chile and transfer to a blender.

4  Add fresh poblano chile, tomatillo, garlic, olive oil, and salt. Puree until nearly smooth.

5  Transfer to a small bowl and serve.

Ricardo James

41

# PLATFORMS

As stated in the introduction of this book, a platform is the delivery mechanism used in Mexican cuisine. It allows you to enjoy the delicate fillings and tangy toppings without an overbearing flavor. It provides a package so that eating with your hands is less messy. A tightly rolled corn tortilla can be used as a platform for frijoles or soup. Meat-filled tortillas form enchiladas. Fried flat tortillas make tostadas, a perfect platform for tinga. Fried cut tortillas, or totopos, are used in chilaquiles and ceviche. The list is endless, as are the fillings described in the Main Dishes chapter.

In the following pages are seven platforms I believe to be the basis for most home- and street-prepared Mexican food: pan, corn tortillas, flour tortillas, sopes, gorditas, totopos, and tamales. Each lends itself to countless recipes that, once mastered, will fill your kitchen with the smells of Mexico.

# PAN

## Bread

Bread, or pan in Spanish, is a unique element to Mexican cuisine. I won't say that Mexicans never bake, but they visit the bakery more frequently than they open their ovens (if they even have one).

With that in mind, I wanted to touch on pan only for the sake of acknowledging its importance as a platform. The local bakery in most Mexican neighborhoods offers many sweet delights that are less sweet than our baked goods in the United States. The more commonly consumed

pan is the bolillo or telera: a soft oval roll perfectly sized for sandwiches or tortas.

Bolillos are inexpensive and are baked daily. They are as common as sliced white bread.

Enjoy the recipes in chapter five that incorporate pan in several sandwiches.

# TORTILLAS DE MAÍZ

## Corn Tortillas | Time: 20 minutes

*The corn tortilla is the main staple in Mexican cuisine. It finds its way to the table more often than not. It is served at breakfast, lunch, and dinner. Warm, freshly made tortillas are nothing like the cardboard-tasting versions you buy in the grocery store. Sadly, we buy those packaged tortillas all too often—me included. These tortillas are so easy and quick, I promise you'll love them. There's no excuse for cardboard again!*

**1 cup corn flour for tortillas**

**¼ tsp. salt**

**¾ cup warm water**

**Makes 8 tortillas**

1 Prepare to make tortillas:

- With scissors, cut off the bottom seam and the handles of a plastic grocery bag. This leaves you with a plastic tube. Cut one side of the tube, making a single sheet of plastic, removing any plastic with printing. Trim the plastic, leaving a 10-inch by 20-inch rectangle.

- Locate your tortilla press. (If you don't have a press, use a heavy skillet or flat dinner plate.)

- Locate a thin metal spatula.

- Heat a comal or electric griddle to 300 degrees. (A comal is a stovetop griddle made of cast iron. A comal evenly distributes the heat and can be used on an electric or gas stove.)

2 In a large bowl, combine the tortilla flour and salt.

3 Add water and mix with a fork until clumpy.

**CONTINUED ON NEXT PAGE**

**4** Knead with your hand until all the flour is incorporated into a single ball of dough. Knead for about 1 minute. The dough should be soft and pliable.

**5** Form into eight 1¼-inch balls.

**6** Line your tortilla press with the plastic rectangle.

**7** Place a ball of dough in the center of the bottom side of the tortilla press. Fold the plastic over and close the tortilla press. Press down with heavy force. (If you don't have a press, you may have to exert a little more force.)

**8** Check the tortilla for thickness. It should be approximately 1/16 inch thick and 6 inches in diameter.

**9** Peel off the top side of the plastic. Place your left hand over the tortilla (assuming you are right handed). Lift the bottom plastic to invert the tortilla onto your hand. Peel the plastic off the tortilla.

**10** Place your right hand perpendicular halfway through the tortilla. Transfer the tortilla to your right hand. This should leave half of the tortilla dangling off the left side of your right hand.

**11** Lay the dangling end of the tortilla on the hot griddle and remove your hand from underneath the tortilla to the right.

**12** Cook tortilla for 30 seconds. With a thin metal spatula, flip the tortilla over and cook an additional 30 seconds. Do not overcook. It should be pliable, not dry.

**13** Remove tortilla from the griddle and store in a tortilla warmer or in a clean folded dish towel.

**14** Repeat tortilla-making steps for other balls of dough.

**NOTE** *If you let your griddle sit too long, it will get too hot and your tortilla will be dry. Keep the heat just under 300 degrees.*

47

# TORTILLAS DE HARINA

## Flour Tortillas | Time: 40 minutes

*I lived in northern Mexico for a short stint, where I grew accustomed to the flour tortilla. It is as common as white bread is in America. The corn tortilla takes a backseat in northern Mexico. Similar to the corn tortillas, homemade flour tortillas are nothing like those you can buy in the store. The homemade tortilla is lighter, flakier, and richer in flavor. However, homemade tortillas are best fresh and don't last until the next day. Tip: Keep plenty of lard on hand.*

**2¾ cups flour, plus more**

**2 tsp. salt**

**⅔ cup lard**

**¾ cup cool tap water**

**Makes 16 medium or 12 large tortillas**

**1** Preheat a griddle to 250 degrees.

**2** Combine flour and salt in a food processor and pulse a few times. Add the lard and pulse until fully combined.

**3** Slowly but constantly add the water and process for 1 complete minute. Dough should be soft and pliable. Divide into 16 balls for medium tortillas, or 12 if you want larger tortillas.

**4** Using a rolling pin and a bit of flour, roll out each ball into an 8-inch tortilla. Don't worry if they are not perfectly round—this takes lots of practice, and in the end they all taste the same.

**5** After rolling a tortilla out, transfer it to the hot griddle and cook for approximately 45 seconds. Flip and cook for another 30 seconds. Using a spatula, keep the large bubbles down. You may need to flip several times so it gets evenly cooked.

**6** Remove and keep warm in a clean dish towel.

**7** Repeat steps for all tortillas.

48

# SOPES

## Corn and Potato Boats | Time: 45 minutes

*Sopes are a perfect example of this book's theme and the use of platforms in Mexican cuisine. Sopes are like little boats with sides that contain the filling. They can be bite-size or up to 5 inches in diameter. I prepare mine about 2½ inches—more than a bite but easy to eat. Sopes can be filled with any type of filling.*

**1 medium potato, peeled and cubed**

**water for boiling**

**1 cup corn flour for tortillas**

**1 tsp. salt**

**1 cup water**

**vegetable oil**

**Makes 10 sopes**

1  Heat a comal or griddle to 275 degrees. (A comal is a stovetop griddle made of cast iron. A comal evenly distributes the heat and can be used on an electric or gas stove.)

2  Place the cubed potato in a medium saucepan and cover with water. Simmer until soft.

3  Drain the potato and transfer to a large bowl. Add the corn flour, salt, and 1 cup water.

4  Mix with a potato masher until it forms a dough. No need to knead.

5  Form into 10 balls.

6  With wet hands, press a ball, transferring it between hands until you have a disc ⅓ inch thick and 3 inches in diameter.

7  Place the sope on the hot griddle and cook for approximately 1 minute.

8  Flip and cook an additional minute. The center of the sope will be slightly undercooked.

**9** Repeat steps with the remaining sopes.

**NOTE** *At this point you may store the sopes in an airtight container for up to 2 days in the refrigerator. When you plan to finish the sopes, remove from the refrigerator and bring to room temperature.*

**10** Heat the oil in a large frying pan to 325 degrees.

**11** Using your thumbs to form the ridge around the edge of the sope, break the surface, press from the center of the sope, and pinch to the edge. Make sure not to break a hole in the bottom. Rotate the sope and repeat until you have a ridge all the way around.

**12** Repeat with remaining sopes.

**13** Fry several sopes at a time in the hot oil. The outside should be golden and crispy but the middle should be tender.

**14** Drain on paper towels.

# GORDITAS

Little Fat Cakes | Time: 25 minutes

**1 medium potato, peeled and cubed**

**water for boiling**

**1 cup corn flour for tortillas**

**1 tsp. salt**

**1 cup water**

**vegetable oil**

**Makes 10 gorditas**

**1** Heat a comal or griddle to 275 degrees.

**2** Place the cubed potato in a medium saucepan and cover with water. Simmer until soft.

**3** Drain the potato and transfer to a large bowl. Add the corn flour, salt, and 1 cup water.

**4** Mix with a potato masher until it forms a dough. No need to knead.

**5** Form into 10 balls.

**6** With wet hands, press a ball, transferring it between hands until you have a disc 1/3 inch thick and 3 inches in diameter.

**7** Place the gordita on the hot griddle and cook for approximately 1½ minutes.

**8** Flip and cook an additional 1½ minutes. The gordita should be cooked through.

**9** Repeat with the remaining gorditas, set aside, and cool.

**NOTE** *You may store the gorditas in an airtight container for up to 2 days in the refrigerator. Suggestions for gordita fillings are found in the main dish chapter (p. 103).*

53

# TOTOPOS

## Chips | Time: 25 minutes

*Totopo comes from the Aztec word tlaxcaltotopochtl. It literally means "tortilla that makes thunder" because they are noisy when you eat them. You could always buy your favorite corn chips, but our family likes this rustic method of chips that uses less fat. Enjoy these with any topping.*

**7 store-bought corn tortillas**

**cooking spray**

**salt for sprinkling**

**chile powder for sprinkling, such as cayenne, árbol, or pequín**

**Makes 42 chips**

**1** Heat an oven to 325 degrees.

**2** Cut the tortillas into 6 pie piece–shaped triangles.

**3** Spray a baking sheet with cooking spray (I prefer sprays made of natural oils).

**4** Spread the chips out in a single layer on the baking sheet and lightly coat chips with cooking spray.

**5** Sprinkle with salt and your favorite chile powder—you determine the amount of heat.

**6** Bake on the middle rack for 7–10 minutes. Flip and bake an additional 3–4 minutes. Chips should be crispy.

Ricardo James

# MASA DE TAMALES

## Tamale Dough | Time: 20 minutes

*Most Mexican families enjoy tamales during Navidad (Christmas season). The weekend after Thanksgiving, I make a point to make a large batch of tamales that will last us through the holidays. We usually make both green and red pork tamales, but our family favors red tamales. Once made, you can freeze tamales in bundles of 10–12 for cooking later in the steamer.*

*For ease of use, I purchase prepared masa from my local Mexican market.*

**2 cups corn flour for tamales**

**½ tsp. salt**

**1 tsp. baking powder**

**2 cups water**

**1 cup shortening**

**Makes enough dough for 8 tamales**

1  Combine corn flour, salt, and baking powder in a large mixing bowl.

2  Add water and mix with a fork until you have a soft dough.

3  In a small bowl using a hand mixer, beat shortening until fluffy.

4  Transfer the shortening to the bowl with the flour mixture and beat with hand mixer until well incorporated. The dough should be soft and light yellow.

5  Store dough in an airtight container in the refrigerator for up to 1 week.

# MAIN DISHES

## Platos Fuertes

**W**ith basics and platforms understood, we will now explore the plato fuerte, strong plate or main dish. The basics provide sauces, flavorings, and toppings to each dish. The platforms are interchangeable among most delectable recipes. My suggestions are merely that: ideas to help you create your own favorite combinations.

As I have stated, I present authentic Mexican food and stay true to the ingredients and flavors. But that doesn't mean a deviation here or there won't become your favorite. Enjoy, mix and match, and share your creations with the ones you love!

# QUESO FUNDIDO CON CHORIZO

## Melted Cheese and Sausage | Time: 20 minutes

In the neighborhood of Lomas de Chapultepec in Mexico City sits a quaint restaurant that serves traditional Mexican fare. In the middle of each table is a small hibachi-type grill with a comal on top. (A comal is a stovet turnop griddle made of cast iron.) I can't resist but order the queso fundido when I frequent this place. I love the melty cheese and the smoky chorizo. Handmade tortillas accompany the guacamole and the salsas. In this recipe I try to bring back those flavors that I crave when I'm there.

½ lb. chorizo sausage

1 medium white onion, halved and sliced

1 pepper, sliced (red, yellow, or green pepper—for more heat choose poblano or anaheim)

3 cups shredded manchego or chihuahua cheese

salt

## TOPPINGS

salsa

guacamole

white onions, diced

cilantro, chopped

Makes 6 servings

1. Remove the casings from the chorizo and fry in frying pan over medium-high heat. Break into small pieces as it cooks. Add the onion and your choice of peppers and sauté until onion and peppers are wilted and soft.

2. Assemble queso fundido in 6 small oven-proof dishes: Spread ½ cup cheese in each dish, sprinkle with salt, and top with chorizo mixture.

3. Broil for 10 minutes on top rack or until cheese is bubbling.

4. Prepare toppings in individual bowls for serving.

5. Serve immediately while hot.

NOTE *If you can't find authentic Mexican cheeses, try monterey jack, cheddar, or mozzarella.*

Ricardo James

# PICADILLO

## Taco Filling | Time: 30 minutes

*The word* picadillo *simply means "minced filling." It usually refers to a ground beef–based taco filling with onions and potatoes. This recipe is great in tacos, gorditas, burritos, or a casserole.*

1 lb. ground beef

1 potato, diced

1 cup water

1 small white onion, diced

2 tomatoes, chopped

½ cup green olives, minced

½ cup raisins

2 cloves garlic, minced

½ tsp. ground clove

½ tsp. ground cinnamon

¼ cup cilantro, chopped

1 tsp. salt

**Makes 8 servings**

1  Brown the beef in a large pot. Drain the grease. Return to heat.

2  Add potato and water. Cover and simmer on low for 5 minutes.

3  Add remaining ingredients. Add more water if needed. Simmer for an additional 10 minutes.

4  Serve on your favorite platform; I prefer tacos or gorditas.

# TAMALES DE PUERCO

Pork Tamales
Time: 90 minutes and 5-hour cooking time

*One of our family's traditional Christmas foods is tamales. We make a point the weekend after Thanksgiving to make a large batch of tamales that will last us through the holidays. We usually make both green and red chile pork tamales, but our family favorite is the red version. Once made, you can freeze them in bundles of ten to twelve for cooking later in the steamer.*

1 large pork roast
  (5- to 7-lb. pork butt)

1 quart water

1 Tbsp. salt

2 Tbsp. dried oregano

4 cups enchilada sauce,
  divided (page 22)

7–8 dozen dried corn husks

10 lbs. tamale masa, room
  temperature (page 57)

1 Tbsp. salt

Makes 50–60 tamales

## PREPARING THE PORK

1  Place the pork roast in a large slow cooker with water, salt, and oregano. Slow cook for 4 hours.

2  Debone and defat pork, then shred into a very large bowl. Add 3 cups Enchilada Sauce and mix well. Set aside.

## ASSEMBLING THE TAMALES

3  Separate all the husks from each other into a clean sink. Fill the sink with warm water. Use a heavy lid to keep them submerged for at least 20 minutes.

4  Place the Tamale Masa in a large bowl and add salt and remaining enchilada sauce. Mix until fully incorporated.

5  Drain the husks and rinse them. Place them in a third large bowl.

6  Take a large husk and place it on the counter or table in front of you with the slick side up and the small end pointed away from you.

CONTINUED ON NEXT PAGE

65

**7** With a spatula, spread ½ cup masa on the large end of the husk, centering a 3-inch square of dough between the sides. The masa should run along the bottom edge.

**8** Place 2–3 tablespoons of chile pork down the middle of the tamale. Roll the tamale from one side to the other, encasing the pork with masa. Fold up the small end of the husk. If I plan to cook the tamales right away, I will only wrap them once, leaving the tops open. If I am going to freeze them and steam them at a later date, I double-wrap them. For a decorative touch, you can tie them with a small strip of husk or twine.

**9** Repeat this about 5 dozen times until you run out of masa or pork or both.

**NOTE** *Unfortunately, it is easy to let the water evaporate completely when steaming tamales. I avoid this problem by placing a nickel in the bottom of the steamer. While there is water, the nickel rattles. When I can't hear the nickel, it alerts me to add more water.*

66

Ricardo James

**10** To cook the tamales, place them in a large steamer folded-side down (I use a very large pasta pot with an inserted colander). If you don't need a full pot, place a metal or glass bowl in half of the pot so that the tamales stand up. Cover with extra husks to keep in the steam.

**11** Steam over low boiling water for 45–60 minutes. For years I overcooked my tamales. They are so much better when they are soft. After 40 minutes, check the doneness of the tamales by removing one and unrolling it. If the husk comes away clean and the middle of the tamale is not soft or watery, then your tamale is done. Remove from the heat and leave covered until ready to serve.

**12** Serve with your favorite toppings, which could include green chile, enchilada sauce, salsa, cheese, sour cream—you get the idea.

**NOTE** *I once could not find corn husks, so I used coffee filters. They worked!*

# TINGA DE POLLO

## Chicken Hash | Time: 45 minutes

*Our family's favorite food! Tinga is eaten in central Mexico primarily as street food. The word* tinga *essentially means hash, so really tinga can be made of anything. In Mexico, however, it is usually made with chicken and onions in a chipotle adobo sauce. My kids always ask for tinga on their birthdays or other special occasions—it truly is their favorite.*

1 roasted chicken, deboned (page 32)

2 Tbsp. vegetable oil

3 large white onions; peeled, halved, and sliced

1 tsp. salt

1 can tomato sauce

1 can chipotles

¾ cup chicken broth or water

½ pint sour cream

20 tostada shells

1 cup crumbled cotija cheese

**Makes 20 tostadas**

1   Cool and shred the chicken. Set aside.

2   In a large dutch oven or pot, heat the oil on medium high.

3   Add the sliced onions and salt. Cook for 8–10 minutes, until the onions get soft but not mushy.

4   Meanwhile, in a blender, puree the tomato sauce and chipotles with broth or water.

5   Add the chicken to the onions and add the chile puree through a strainer.

6   Simmer for 10 minutes. Add more salt if needed. If saving for later, transfer the tinga to a slow cooker and keep warm on low.

7   To serve, dab a little sour cream on each tostada shell and evenly spread to the edges.

8   Top each shell with ½ cup of tinga and sprinkle with cotija cheese.

**NOTE**   *Tinga is super versatile. As with most fillings, it can be eaten in tacos, in gorditas, or on tostadas. My family also enjoys it spread on tortilla chips in nachos, topped with sour cream and cotija cheese.*

Ricardo James

Ricardo James

# CEVICHE DE CAMARÓN

## Mexican Shrimp Cocktail
Time: 30 minutes and 2-hour marinate time

*This is such a great party food! Your friends will request it over and over. Ceviche is the process by which seafood and shellfish are cooked by acid. This recipe uses shrimp in lime juice. You'll get a lot more flavor if you use raw shrimp and actually "cook" it in the lime juice before proceeding. However, in a pinch, you can take a shortcut and use pre-cooked shrimp.*

2 lbs. raw shrimp; peeled, deveined, and tails removed

juice of 10–12 limes

1 large English cucumber, peeled and diced

1 large white onion, diced and rinsed in cold water

1 small jícama, peeled and chopped

1 cup diced celery

½ cup cilantro, chopped

1 cup ketchup

½ cup hot sauce (I prefer Valentina brand)

juice of 2 limes

1 tsp. salt

2 avocados, pitted and diced

corn chips or saltine crackers

**Serves 10**

1 Cut shrimp into bite-size pieces.

**NOTE** *I prefer a small chop when serving at a party with chips, and larger pieces when serving in glass cups.*

2 In a nonmetallic bowl, mix shrimp and lime juice. Refrigerate for 2 hours to "cook." Stir occasionally. The shrimp will have completed the cooking process when the pieces are entirely white and no longer translucent.

3 Drain shrimp and add cucumber, onion, jícama, celery, and cilantro. Toss.

4 In a separate bowl, mix the ketchup, hot sauce, additional lime juice, and salt. Pour the sauce over the ceviche and mix well. Refrigerate until ready to eat.

**NOTE** *To make less hot, use more ketchup and less hot sauce.*

5 Add the avocados just before serving. Toss gently.

6 Serve with corn tortilla chips or saltine crackers. Mexicans eat ceviche in a cocktail glass.

# CAMARONES AHOGADOS EN MOLE

## Drunken Shrimp in Mole | Time: 15 minutes

*The mole adds smokiness and extreme flavor to the shrimp. The lime juice cuts the mole's richness and adds tanginess. It makes a perfect appetizer.*

2 Tbsp. cooking oil

1 lb. shrimp, peeled and deveined

juice of 2 limes

1/3 cup mole poblano (page 20)

pickled red onions (page 37)

Serves 4

1  Heat the oil in a large frying pan on medium high.

2  Fry the shrimp until cooked through.

3  Add lime juice and mole. Toss until thoroughly coated.

4  Transfer to a serving plate. Top with onions.

5  Serve immediately.

**NOTE**  *I leave the tails on the shrimp. They make great handles if eating with your fingers.*

# CEVICHE DE TRUCHA ARCOIRIS CON PIÑA

Rainbow Trout with Pineapple Cocktail
Time: 20 minutes and 2-hour marinate time

*Most flaky fish can be made into ceviche. Try snapper, halibut, or salmon. I have an ample supply of rainbow trout because my neighbor is an avid trout fisherman. We enjoy this ceviche on a regular basis. Ceviche is the technique by which fish is "cooked" by the acid of freshly squeezed juice of one or more citrus fruits.*

1 cup fish—skin and bone removed, cut into even bite-size pieces

juice of 10 limes

1 cup diced fresh pineapple

2 poblano chiles; peeled, cleaned, and diced

½ tsp. chile pequín powder

½ tsp. salt

10 tostada shells

## TOPPING

1 large red onion, thinly sliced

1 cup white vinegar

1 Tbsp. sugar

½ tsp. dried oregano

Makes 10 tostadas

1   In a nonmetallic bowl, marinate fish in lime juice for 2 hours.

2   Meanwhile, mix pineapple and prepared chiles. Set aside.

3   Soak onion slices in vinegar with sugar and oregano. Set aside.

4   Drain fish and add to pineapple and chiles. Toss with chile powder and salt.

5   To assemble, place ¼ cup ceviche on each tostada. Top with drained red onions.

NOTE   *You can serve ceviche as a dip at a party with totopos (page 54).*

# QUESADILLAS

## Cheese Pockets | Time: 20 minutes

*Contrary to popular belief, true quesadillas are made with corn tortillas—homemade tortillas, to be exact. They can also be fried in a little oil if you want them crispy. You can add a filling for a little extra flavor, or serve with your favorite salsa.*

**8 corn tortillas**
**(page 45)**

**1 cup melting cheese**
**(manchego or chihuahua)**

**2 Tbsp. oil (optional)**

**Suggested toppings:**
**chili beans (page 28),**
**guacamole (page 18),**
**green salsa (page 14),**
**salsa de chile (page 12)**

**Makes 8 quesadillas**

1 Heat a comal or griddle to 300 degrees. (A comal is a stovetop griddle made of cast iron. A comal evenly distributes the heat and can be used on an electric or gas stove.)

2 Warm a tortilla on both sides. Place a generous amount of cheese on one half.

3 Fold the tortilla over the cheese and press with a spatula.

4 Cook until cheese is melted, flipping from side to side.

5 If desired, in a small frying pan, heat 2 tablespoons oil on medium heat. Fry each side of the quesadilla until crispy.

6 Serve warm.

77

# SINCRONIZADAS

## Cheese Pockets with Ham | Time: 20 minutes

*What we refer to in the United States as a quesadilla is actually a sincronizada. Usually made with a flour tortilla, it contains ham along with cheese.*

**8 homemade flour tortillas (page 48)**

**1 cup melting cheese (manchego or chihuahua)**

**8 slices deli ham**

**salsa or guacamole**

**Makes 8 sincronizadas**

1. Heat a comal or griddle to 300 degrees.

2. Warm a tortilla on both sides. Place a generous amount of cheese on one half.

3. Top with a slice of ham.

4. Fold the tortilla over the cheese and press with a spatula.

5. Cook until cheese is melted, flipping from side to side.

6. Repeat for all tortillas.

7. Serve warm with your favorite salsa or guacamole.

78

# HUEVOS RANCHEROS

## Ranch Eggs | Time: 60 minutes

*This dish has become our Sunday morning favorite!*

*Huevos rancheros is rather complex. The cooking techniques are not difficult, but the assembly process must be organized. They are best prepared to order. However, they are well worth the work. This is not the kind of meal that everyone can eat together—I fix one plate at a time for whoever is ready.*

**4–5 strips bacon, chopped**

**4 cups refried beans (page 26)**

**2–3 cups enchilada sauce (page 22)**

**½ cup vegetable oil**

**olive oil**

**butter**

**16 corn tortillas**

**16 eggs**

**1 cup crumbled cotija cheese**

**1 medium white onion, diced and rinsed in cold water**

**1 cup sour cream**

**16 cooked bacon strips for garnish**

**Makes 8 servings**

1 Fry the chopped bacon in a large frying pan until crispy. Add refried beans and simmer until warm. Keep warm.

2 Warm the enchilada sauce.

3 Prepare 2 frying pans, one for tortillas, the other for eggs. In the one for tortillas, put vegetable oil and heat. In the one for eggs put a teaspoon of olive oil and a small dab of butter.

4 Quickly fry a tortilla until soft/chewy, 10–12 seconds, turning after 8 seconds.

5 Cook 2 eggs at a time to your liking.

Ricardo James

## 6  ASSEMBLY

Put ⅓–½ cup Refried Beans on plate.

Top beans with 2 cooked tortillas.

Top tortillas with prepared eggs.

Top eggs with ¼ cup Enchilada Sauce.

Top with crumbled cotija cheese.

Top with diced white onions.

Add a dollop of sour cream.

Garnish with bacon strips.

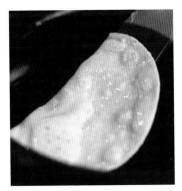

**7**  Repeat frying the tortillas and eggs, and the assembly, until everyone is full.

# CHILAQUILES

## Spicy Drowned Tortilla Chips with Chicken
## Time: 45 minutes

*A typical Mexican breakfast will often include chilaquiles. Its origin comes from peasant food and the leftover scraps or totopos (chips) from the day before—old tortillas torn into pieces and fried, leftover salsa, and some leftover chicken pieces. It is pretty much the same on our table.*

cooking oil

**9 tortillas (day old), each cut into 6 pie piece–shaped pieces**

**3 cups enchilada sauce (page 22)**

**2 cups shredded roasted chicken (page 32)**

**2 cups shredded melting cheese, such as manchego or chihuahua**

**½ medium white onion, sliced**

**sour cream**

**Makes 6–8 servings**

1 Heat ½ inch of oil in a large pan.

2 Fry day-old tortilla pieces until crisp. Drain on a paper towel and set aside.

3 Heat enchilada sauce and keep warm.

**NOTE** *You may choose to prepare individual portions separately or all together in a casserole dish. I prefer the texture of the tortillas when prepared individually. When made into a casserole, the tortillas tend to be more soggy. I like them more chewy.*

4 Layer sauce, chicken, tortillas, and cheese in oven-safe dish(es). Repeat layers 2 more times.

5 Top with cheese and broil for 3 minutes until the cheese is melted.

6 Garnish with sliced onions and sour cream.

# CHILE VERDE

## Green Chile Sauce | Time: 4 hours

*This makes a great Sunday dinner. It can be used in tacos, burritos, or nachos, or you can do what we do and put it on sopes (see page 86).*

1¼ cups lard, divided

2 lbs. pork roast, cubed in 1-inch pieces

3 quarts plus 1¼ cups water, divided

3 tsp. salt, divided

2 large white onions, chopped, divided

1 red pepper, chopped

6 large tomatillos, chopped

8 jalapeño peppers, sliced, divided

8 cloves garlic, mashed

2 medium potatoes, peeled and cubed

4 medium carrots, peeled and sliced

32-oz. canned green chiles, diced

½ cup flour

1 (14-oz.) can stewed tomatoes

**Makes about 2 gallons**

1 Heat 1 cup lard in large frying pan on medium high.

2 Working in batches, fry the pork pieces until golden brown on all sides. Be careful not to burn the grease—it will be used later. As you fry the pork, transfer it to the pot (see next step).

3 Heat 3 quarts water and 2 teaspoons salt in a 10-quart pot.

4 In the oil left from frying the meat, fry 1 of the chopped onions, red pepper, tomatillos, 2 of the jalapeño peppers, garlic, and 1 teaspoon salt until vegetables are medium soft.

5 Transfer everything from the frying pan to the pot. Put ¼ cup water into the frying pan. Using a spatula, scrape the bottom and sides of the pan to collect the extra pieces of fried food and add contents to the pot. Simmer covered on low for 1 hour.

6 With a slotted spoon and pair of tongs, remove the meat from the pot and set aside.

7 Puree the vegetables in the pot with a hand blender or potato masher.

84

Ricardo James

**8** Return meat to the pot. Add potatoes, carrots, green chiles, and 1 cup water. Simmer on low for 30 minutes.

**9** In a large frying pan, heat remaining ¼ cup lard. Sauté second chopped onion and remaining 6 jalapeño peppers until tender.

**10** Sprinkle ½ cup flour over the vegetables and continue to sauté for 3 minutes. The flour will stick to the vegetables and become golden.

**11** Add contents of the pan to the pot, using a whisk to incorporate completely.

**12** Add stewed tomatoes.

**13** Taste. Add additional salt if necessary. Simmer for 30 minutes on low, stirring occasionally to keep from burning. Keep warm in a slow cooker, store in the refrigerator, or freeze to use later.

· · · · · · · · · · · · · · **My Favorite Uses of Chile Verde** · · · · · · · · · · · · ·

- Smother tamales
- Smother burritos
- Smother homemade french fries with cheese and sour cream
- Mix with sour cream for enchiladas
- In a bowl, served with warm flour tortillas

# SOPES DE FRIJOLES Y CARNITAS

## Sopes with Beans and Roasted Pork
## Time: 30 minutes and 4-hour cooking time

*Sopes are a perfect example of this book's theme and the use of platforms in Mexican cuisine. Sopes are like little boats with sides that help contain the filling. They can be bite-size or up to 5 inches in diameter. I prepare mine about 2½ inches—more than a bite but easy to eat. Sopes can be filled with any type of filling; however, I tend to use this recipe most of the time.*

**1½-lb. pork roast**

**3 cups water**

**1 tsp. salt**

**1 (7-oz.) can salsa ranchera (I prefer Herdez brand)**

**2 cups prepared pot beans (page 24)**

**12–15 sopes (page 50)**

### POSSIBLE TOPPINGS

**chile verde (page 84)**

**salsa ranchera (page 11)**

**queso fresco**

**shredded lettuce**

**shredded cabbage**

Makes 12–15 sopes

1 Place pork roast in a slow cooker with 3 cups water. Sprinkle with salt. Pour salsa over the meat.

2 Slow cook for 3 hours. Pork will be very tender.

3 Shred the pork. Return to pot with the juices. Keep warm.

4 Prepare sopes. Warm them if necessary.

5 Top with beans, shredded pork, and favorite toppings.

Ricardo James

# ENCHILADAS SUIZAS

## Swiss Enchiladas | Time: 60 minutes

*Enchiladas Suizas are an everyday classic, are easy to make, and are topped with a light green sauce made from pureed vegetables. These enchiladas were influenced by Swiss immigrants to Mexico, who established dairies to produce cream and cheese. The spinach, onions, green salsa, and cream give it a unique flavor.*

### GREEN CREAM SAUCE

2 small zucchinis, chopped

1 medium white onion, chopped

6 tomatillos, chopped

2 serrano chiles, chopped

2 cloves garlic, chopped

1 Tbsp. cooking oil

1 tsp. salt

3 cups fresh spinach, chopped

¼ cup cilantro, chopped

2 (4-oz.) cans diced green chiles

1 cup crema Mexicana (page 35), or sour cream

1½ cups water

8–10 corn tortillas (page 45)

1 roasted chicken, shredded (page 32)

2 cups shredded quesadilla cheese (jack cheese will work)

### TOPPINGS

queso fresco cheese, crumbled

1 medium white onion, sliced

crema Mexicana or sour cream

Makes 8–10 enchiladas

1   Preheat broiler oven to high.

2   Spread zucchinis, onion, tomatillos, chiles, and garlic on a baking sheet. Toss with cooking oil and sprinkle with salt.

## CONTINUED ON NEXT PAGE

**3** Roast under the broiler until charring begins, then remove. Turn oven to bake and set temperature to 325 degrees.

**4** Puree cooked vegetables, spinach, cilantro, green chiles, and crema Mexicana (or sour cream) in a blender until smooth.

**5** Heat the water in a frying pan on very low.

**6** Ladle 1½ cups prepared green sauce into the bottom of the baking dish.

**7** Soften a tortilla by submerging in the water for a few seconds. If you leave it too, long it will turn to mush.

**8** Remove tortilla and place on a clean work surface. Lay ¼ cup shredded chicken and a portion of shredded cheese across the middle.

**9** Roll tightly. Lay in the baking dish, seam side down.

**10** Repeat for all tortillas until your baking dish is full.

**11** Cover enchiladas with remaining green sauce. Bake for 30 minutes.

**12** When serving, sprinkle with crumbled cheese and sliced onions. Drizzle with crema Mexicana or sour cream.

# TACOS AL PASTOR

Shepherd's Tacos
Time: 20 minutes, 6-hour marinate time,
         15-minute cook time

*Tacos al pastor is a masterful piece of cooking. It is essentially the Mexican version of the Greek gyro or the Lebanese shawarma—a marinated meat cooked on a rotisserie. Tacos al pastor came about when Lebanese immigrants relocated to Mexico City in the nineteenth century. It is almost always made of pork with a touch of pineapple. Recipes vary widely, and a good pastor recipe is held secret by restaurants. Here is my version. If you have an end-on-end rotisserie, then by all means go for it. Marinating takes at least 3 hours. This recipe is rather complex but is well worth it at a big party.*

## MARINADE

**NOTE** *The marinade can be made ahead of time and stored in the refrigerator or freezer.*

2 cups enchilada sauce (page 22)

½ (7-oz.) can chipotle chiles in adobo sauce, pureed with ½ cup water

2 Tbsp. vegetable oil

2 cloves garlic, minced

1 cup pineapple juice

⅔ cup white vinegar

1½ tsp. cinnamon

2½ Tbsp. salt

1 Tbsp. Mexican oregano

5 lbs. boneless pork butt, chopped into small ½-inch pieces (I ask my butcher to do this)

2 medium white onions, sliced thin

1 pineapple; cleaned, cored and chopped

## TOPPINGS

cilantro, minced

white onion, diced

lime wedges

salsa verde (page 14)

guacamole (page 18)

40 mini or regular corn tortillas

Feeds 10–12 people

1  In a large bowl, combine enchilada sauce, chipotles, oil, garlic, pineapple juice, vinegar, cinnamon, salt, and oregano.

2  Divide pork into 3 large plastic freezer bags.

3  Add ⅓ of the onion and pineapple to each bag.

4  Pour ⅓ of the marinade into each bag. Seal, removing excess air, and massage to coat the meat well.

5  Refrigerate 3–6 hours or overnight.

6  Heat broiler on high.

7  Working in batches, spread the marinated ingredients on a baking sheet in a single layer. Try not to crowd the ingredients. Broil 10–15 minutes, or until charring occurs. If the pork renders excess liquid, pour off the liquid and return to the broiler. Meat should be crispy but tender.

8  Prepare tacos using 2 tortillas so they hold up to hand eating. Place ¼ cup of taco meat and a touch of roasted pineapple, and finish with any combination of toppings.

# TAQUITOS DE PESCADO

## Fried Fish Tacos | Time: 45 minutes

*If you pause to think, Mexican tacos are soft, rolled corn tortillas with a filling. Toppings are stuffed inside the taco. Taquitos are filled, rolled corn tacos that are deep fried. The toppings are added to the outside. Shredded beef, chicken, and fish usually find their way into taquitos because they hold up under frying. These crispy delights are a great diversion from the typical taco.*

**2 Tbsp. olive oil**

**½ medium white onion, diced**

**¼ cup cilantro, chopped**

**1 tsp. cumin**

**1 serrano chile, minced**

**½ tsp. salt**

**2 cups fresh fish in chunks (choose a fish that is flaky in texture, such as snapper, halibut, or salmon)**

**½ cup prepared enchilada sauce (page 22)**

**3 cups vegetable oil**

**10–12 corn tortillas**

**Makes 10–12 taquitos**

1 In a large frying pan, heat the olive oil on medium. Add onion, cilantro, cumin, chile, and salt. Sauté for 2 minutes.

2 Add fish. Carefully sauté, so as to not break up the fish, until the fish is flaky, about 5 minutes.

3 Add enchilada sauce. Toss gently. Remove from heat and cover.

4 Heat the vegetable oil in a large frying pan to 325 degrees. You don't want the oil to be too hot.

5 Fry each tortilla in the oil for 6 seconds on each side. Remove and place on a stack of paper towels to remove the excess oil.

6 When cool enough to handle, place 2 heaping tablespoons of fish filling onto each tortilla and roll tightly.

7 Using toothpicks, secure each taquito in the middle and both ends.

**NOTE** *Taquitos can be rolled several hours ahead of frying.*

Ricardo James

**8** Heat oil to medium high. Fry 3–4 taquitos in the pan until golden and mostly crisp, about 2 minutes. Do not overcook—the tortillas should be crispy but not hard.

**9** Remove and place on a stack of paper towels to remove the excess oil.

**10** Serve with guacamole, sour cream, lettuce, and/or green chile sauce.

# TORTA DE CHORIZO Y HUEVO

## Chorizo and Egg Sandwich | Time: 60 minutes

*Tortas are the Mexican version of sandwiches, and like sandwiches, they are a very popular street food and can be found on many a picnic; easily made at home, they are wrapped in a napkin and packed in a cooler. Mexicans love pickled jalapeños on their tortas. Some of the most popular tortas are made of milanesa (breaded beef steak), pierna (pork), huevos y chorizo (eggs and chorizo sausage), salchichas (hot dog), and cheese. Traditionally, a torta contains a mix of the following condiments: mayonnaise, cheese, avocado or guacamole, tomatoes, jalapeños, and refried beans.*

*Note: Tortas are also great toasted. You can use a griddle or a panini press.*

**½-lb. chorizo sausage**

**½ medium white onion, diced**

**1 large potato, diced**

**½ cup water**

**6 bolillos or telera rolls (found in Mexican bakeries)**

**1 cup refried beans (page 26)**

**6 eggs**

**mayonnaise**

**1 cup guacamole (page 18)**

**½ lb. queso fresco, sliced**

**sliced tomatoes (optional)**

**sliced jalapeños (optional)**

**salt to taste**

**Makes 6 sandwiches**

1 Fry the chorizo in a large frying pan, breaking up the large pieces.

2 Add the onions, potatoes, and water. Cook until potatoes are tender.

3 Slice the bolillo rolls in half to make sandwiches.

4 Heat the refried beans until warm and spreadable.

5 Scramble the eggs in a large frying pan and set aside.

6 Spread refried beans on the bottom piece of bread. Spread mayonnaise and guacamole on the top piece.

7 Spoon the chorizo potato mixture on the beans and press down so that it sticks.

8 Top with queso fresco and scrambled eggs. Add tomatoes and jalapeños if desired. Salt to taste.

Ricardo James

Main Dishes

# TORTA DE JAMÓN Y QUESO

## Ham and Cheese Sandwich | Time: 60 minutes

*This is the most inexpensive and easy way to prepare a torta and is great for picnics.*

**6 bolillo or telera rolls**

**1 cup refried beans (page 26)**

**mayonnaise**

**1 cup guacamole (page 18)**

**½ lb. sliced deli ham**

**½ lb. queso fresco, sliced**

**sliced tomatoes (optional)**

**sliced jalapeños (optional)**

**salt to taste**

**Makes 6 sandwiches**

1 Slice the bolillo rolls in half to make sandwiches.

2 Heat the refried beans until warm and spreadable.

3 Spread refried beans on the bottom piece of bread. Spread mayonnaise and guacamole on the top piece.

4 Layer ham and cheese.

5 Add tomatoes and jalapeños if desired.

6 Salt to taste.

# TACOS DE VERDURAS

## Vegetarian Tacos | Time: 20 minutes

*Squash and mushrooms work well as a replacement for meat. Use this recipe when you want lighter fare or when you have non-meat-eaters present.*

**3 Tbsp. cooking oil**

**1 small zucchini, julienned**

**1 small yellow squash, julienned**

**1 cup portobello mushrooms, chopped**

**1 small white onion, sliced**

**½ tsp. salt**

**¼ tsp. cumin**

**8 corn tortillas (page 45)**

**favorite salsa and toppings**

**Makes 8 tacos**

1  Heat oil in a large pan on medium.

2  Add the vegetables and sprinkle with salt and cumin. Sauté until soft. Set aside.

3  Warm the tortillas on a comal or griddle. Fill tortillas with cooked vegetables and top with your favorite salsa and toppings.

100

Ricardo James

# TACOS DE POLLO ADOBADO A LA PARRILLA

## Grilled Chicken Tacos | Time: 45 minutes

*This is a quick recipe I use in a pinch because it adds a lot of flavor yet requires minimal attention.*

**3 large chicken breasts**

**1 cup hot sauce (I prefer Valentina brand)**

**juice of 4 limes**

**salt**

**12 warm tortillas**

### TOPPINGS

**guacamole (page 18)**

**green salsa (page 14 or 17)**

**salsa ranchera (page 11)**

**cotija cheese, crumbled**

**pickled red onion (page 37)**

Serves 6

1  Heat your gas or charcoal grill.

2  Slightly pound each chicken breast to ½-inch thickness.

3  Place chicken in a large plastic freezer bag. Add hot sauce and lime juice. Close bag and massage to coat. Refrigerate for at least 15 minutes.

4  Grill chicken on each side for 5–8 minutes. Salt as desired.

5  Chop chicken into bite-size pieces suitable for tacos.

6  Place ¼ cup chicken on each warm tortilla. Finish with your favorite toppings.

Ricardo James

# GORDITAS DE FRIJOLES Y QUESO

## Bean and Cheese Corn Pockets | Time: 25 minutes

*Similar to a South American arepa, a gordita is a fat tortilla. They are distinctly different, however—Mexicans make gorditas by transforming the tortilla into a pocket and stuffing it with morsels of delight. This recipe is a simple version with just beans and cheese.*

**8–10 gorditas (page 53)**

**1½ cups pot beans
  (page 24)**

**¾ cup crumbled queso fresco**

**oil**

### TOPPINGS

**guacamole (page 18)**

**green salsa (page 14 or 17)**

**salsa ranchera (page 11)**

**cotija cheese, crumbled**

**crema Mexicana (page 35)
  or sour cream**

Makes 8–10 gorditas

1  Form a pocket in each gordita: using a small serrated knife, split the gordita. With the tip of the knife, deepen the pocket, leaving the 2 halves connected, as shown below.

2  Stuff with 1 tablespoon warm pot beans and a small portion of queso fresco.

3  Heat a frying pan with ¼ inch oil to 325 degrees.

4  Fry the gorditas until crispy on both sides.

5  Serve hot with your favorite toppings.

# ENCHILADAS DE POLLO EN MOLE POBLANO

## Red Mole Chicken Enchiladas | Time: 45 minutes

*I prefer these enchiladas served a la carte, one plate at a time, because that is the traditional way of serving them in Mexico. However, you could prepare them in a casserole dish family style.*

**1 cup water or chicken broth**

**12 corn tortillas (page 45)**

**3 cups shredded roasted chicken (page 32)**

**4 cups prepared mole poblano sauce (page 20)**

**1 cup crema Mexicana (page 35) or sour cream**

**¾ cup queso fresco**

**1 medium white onion, sliced**

Serves 6

1 Heat water or chicken broth in a large frying pan to a simmer.

2 Submerge a tortilla in the liquid for 4 seconds. If you leave it too long, it will turn mushy.

3 Place tortilla on a clean work surface and lay ¼ cup chicken down the center. Wrap tightly and lay in center of a plate. Repeat with a second enchilada.

4 Repeat steps for all enchiladas.

5 Ladle ⅔ cup mole sauce over the enchiladas.

6 Drizzle with crema or sour cream. Sprinkle with queso and top with sliced onions.

7 Serve immediately.

# TAMALES DE CHILE Y QUESO

## Chile and Cheese Tamales
## Time: 90 minutes and I-hour cooking time

*Here is a nonmeat version of the traditional tamale. Tamales are all very similar in prepa-ration. The dough flavoring and the fillings can change, but the rolling and the steaming are the same.*

**2 ancho or poblano chiles, whole**

**4 dozen corn husks**

**NOTE** *The amount of corn husks depends on their size. I've added extra here in case you need to use 2 for each tamale.*

**5 lbs. prepared tamale masa**

**2 tsp. salt**

**1 cup green chile sauce (page 84)**

**1 (½-lb.) block hard cheese, cut into ¼-inch-thick sticks, approximately 3 inches long**

**water for steaming**

**favorite toppings**

**Makes 2 dozen tamales**

1 On a gas grill (or in a broiler set to 500 degrees) roast the chiles for 8–10 minutes. Turn once.

2 Transfer chiles to a paper grocery bag. This will allow the chiles to sweat, making it easier to peel the skins off.

3 After 10 minutes, remove the chiles from the bag and peel off the tough skins. Rinse in a trickle of water to remove seeds. Remove the stems.

4 Cut the chiles into rajas (long, thin strips).

## ASSEMBLING THE TAMALES

5 Separate all the husks from each other into a clean sink. Fill the sink with warm water. Use a heavy lid to keep them sub-merged for at least 20 minutes.

6 Place the tamale masa in a large bowl and add salt and green chile sauce. Mix until fully incorporated.

7 Drain the husks and place them in a third large bowl.

Ricardo James

8 Take a large husk and place it on the counter or table in front of you with the slick side up and the small end pointed away from you.

9 With a spatula, spread ½ cup masa on the large end of the husk, centering a 3-inch square of dough between the sides. The masa should run along the bottom edge.

10 Place 1–2 strips of the chile down the middle of the tamale. Place a stick of cheese with the chile. Roll the tamale from one side to the other, encasing the chile and cheese with masa. Fold up the small end of the husk. Place on the table folded part down.

11 Repeat this about 2 dozen times until you run out of masa or filling or both.

12 To cook the tamales, place them in a steamer folded side down. If you don't need a full pot, place a metal or glass bowl in half of the pot so that the tamales stand up. Cover with extra husks to keep in the steam.

13 Steam over low boiling water for 45–60 minutes. After 40 minutes, check the doneness of the tamales by removing one and unrolling. If the husk comes away clean and the middle of the tamale is not soft or watery, then your tamale is done. Remove from the heat, and leave covered until ready to serve.

14 Serve with your favorite toppings, which could include green chile, enchilada sauce, salsa, cheese, and/or sour cream.

# FIRST COURSES

## Primer Platos

### (Soups, Pastas, and Salads)

**M**ost Americans eat family style. One of the most obvious differences in the way food is presented in Mexico is the concept of a first course, or primer plato ("first plate"). Not an appetizer, the primer plato is a simple dish consisting of a soup, pasta, or salad. When finished, it should leave you hungry for more, thus the plato fuerte ("strong plate") or main dish follows. The primer plato also elongates the meal for more in-depth conversation and pleasantries.

# SOPA DE ALBONDIGAS

## Meatball Soup | Time: 60 minutes

*This simple soup is made in many a Mexican household when the weather turns chilly. Best eaten when freshly made because the meatballs are fragile and easily break.*

### BROTH

2 Tbsp. cooking oil

1 medium white onion, diced

1 celery stalk, diced

2 cloves garlic, minced

1 (14.5-oz.) can diced tomatoes

1 quart chicken broth

1 chicken bouillon cube
(I prefer Knorr brand)

### MEATBALLS

1 lb. lean ground beef

1 egg

¼ cup rice, raw

¼ tsp. cumin

½ tsp. salt

¼ tsp. black pepper

½ tsp. dried oregano

1 tsp. finely chopped fresh mint

1 tsp. finely chopped fresh
parsley

### VEGETABLES

2 cups mixed chopped
vegetables: carrot, potato,
chayote, zucchini, parsnip,
turnip, onion, squash

Serves 8

1   Heat the oil in a large soup pot. Add onion and celery. Sauté for 5 minutes.

2   Add garlic, lower heat, and sweat for an additional 5 minutes.

3   Add tomatoes, broth, and bouillon. Simmer for 10 minutes.

Ricardo James

**4** Using a hand blender, puree the mixture until smooth. (If you like chunkier soup, skip this step.)

**5** Simmer at a low boil while you prepare the meatballs.

**6** In a large bowl, break the ground beef into very small pieces. Add the egg, rice, and spices. Mix with your hands.

**7** Form into 1-inch meatballs and drop into the soup.

**8** Add the vegetables and simmer until tender, about 20 minutes. Be careful when you stir—the meatballs break easily.

# SOPA DE FIDEO

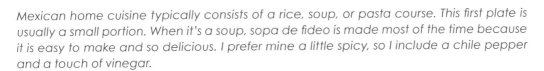

## Noodle Soup | Time: 30 minutes

*Mexican home cuisine typically consists of a rice, soup, or pasta course. This first plate is usually a small portion. When it's a soup, sopa de fideo is made most of the time because it is easy to make and so delicious. I prefer mine a little spicy, so I include a chile pepper and a touch of vinegar.*

1 (14.5-oz.) can diced tomatoes

1 clove garlic, minced

1 serrano or jalapeño chile pepper, chopped (you control the heat)

½ medium white onion, chopped

1 cube chicken bouillon (I prefer Knorr brand)

1 quart chicken broth, divided

2 Tbsp. cooking oil

1 (3- to 4-oz.) pkg. fideo (Mexican noodle pasta)

¼ cup red wine vinegar

### GARNISH

sour cream

cilantro, chopped

Serves 6

1. In a blender, puree tomatoes, garlic, chile, onion, bouillon, and 1 cup of the broth.

2. Heat the oil in a large soup pot over medium heat. Add the fideo and fry until slightly golden. It should only take a minute or two. Remove from the heat.

3. Using a large strainer, add the puree to the warm pot to strain out the chunks.

4. Add the vinegar and remaining broth and simmer on low for 20 minutes until the noodles are soft but not mushy.

5. Serve with a dollop of sour cream and a sprinkle of cilantro.

# SOPA DE POLLO Y VERDURAS

## Chicken Vegetable Soup | Time: 45 minutes

*The first time I had this soup, I was surprised it had fresh avocado. The bigger surprise was how well it tasted. The lime juice adds a freshness and makes it very Mexican.*

**1 quart chicken broth**

**1 jalapeño pepper; halved lengthwise, deseeded, and deveined**

**1 sprig epazote (optional)**

**2 medium carrots, chopped**

**1 chayote, chopped (or use a potato)**

**1 small white onion, diced**

**1 small zucchini, chopped**

**2 cups chopped roasted chicken (page 32)**

**2 vine-ripened tomatoes, chopped and strained**

### TOPPINGS

**1 avocado, pit removed, sliced**

**4 limes, quartered**

**cilantro, chopped**

Serves 6

1  Heat broth, pepper, and epazote to a medium simmer.

2  Add carrots and chayote. Simmer for 8 minutes.

3  Add onion and zucchini. Simmer for an additional 8 minutes.

4  Remove and discard the epazote and jalapeño pepper.

5  Add chicken and tomatoes to the soup. Simmer to heat through.

6  Serve with avocado slices, lime wedges, and a sprinkle of cilantro.

Ricardo James

# POZOLE

## Pork and Hominy Stew
## Time: 45 minutes and 5-hour cooking time

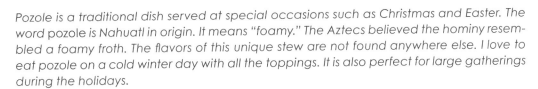

*Pozole is a traditional dish served at special occasions such as Christmas and Easter. The word pozole is Nahuatl in origin. It means "foamy." The Aztecs believed the hominy resembled a foamy froth. The flavors of this unique stew are not found anywhere else. I love to eat pozole on a cold winter day with all the toppings. It is also perfect for large gatherings during the holidays.*

1 lb. pork roast

½ chicken

1 Tbsp. dried oregano

2 tsp. salt

6 cups water

1 large white onion, diced

3 cups enchilada sauce
(page 22)

1 (32-oz.) can hominy, rinsed

### TOPPINGS

radishes, thinly sliced

white onion, diced

cabbage, thinly shredded

lime wedges

dried oregano

red pepper flakes

**Makes 20 servings**

1 Place the pork roast and the chicken into a slow cooker. Cover with water. Add oregano and salt. Cook on low for 3–4 hours.

2 Remove the meat to a plate to cool. Debone, remove fat, and chop into bite-size pieces.

3 Strain the juices from the slow cooker to remove any bones and cartilage. Return the juices to the slow cooker. Add the meat, onion, enchilada sauce, and hominy. Simmer for 1 hour on low.

4 Prepare the table by placing each topping in its own serving dish.

5 Serve pozole in wide bowls to accommodate toppings. Encourage your diners to try them all.

NOTE *Pozole is not complete without the tanginess of the lime and the crunchiness of the vegetables. Use extra oregano and the pepper flakes to add extra flavor and heat.*

# SOPA DE VERDURAS

## Cream of Vegetable Soup | Time: 45 minutes

*Mi amiga, Pera, shared this recipe with my mother. It took me years to coax it out of her. The raw onions are the secret. They brighten the soup yet leave the creaminess of the vegetables intact. Buen provecho!*

**2 carrots, peeled and sliced**

**2 potatoes, peeled and diced**

**2 small zucchini, diced**

**1 celery stalk, diced**

**1 tsp. salt**

**1 medium white onion, diced**

**1 chicken bouillon cube (I prefer Knorr brand)**

salt and pepper

**1 can evaporated milk**

sour cream (optional)

**Makes 6 servings**

1 Place carrots, potatoes, zucchini, and celery in a large soup pot. Add salt, cover with water, and cook until tender.

2 Working in batches, puree the vegetables and liquid in a blender with the raw onion until smooth.

3 Return to the pan. Add bouillon and salt and pepper to taste. Bring to a simmer.

4 Add milk and warm through. Do not boil.

5 Serve with a dollop of sour cream.

Ricardo James

# LASAÑA CON HABANERO CHILE

Habanero Lasagne
Time: 25 minutes and 1-hour cook time

*Tomato-based sauces are common in Mexican cooking. Each cook has favorite ingredients that subtly alter the flavor profile. This sauce uses garlic and habanero chile to add richness and heat. My recipe is vegetarian, but you could add chicken for more protein.*

6 tomatoes, whole

6 cloves garlic, skins on

2 habanero chiles, whole

1 (14.5-oz.) can crushed tomatoes

¼ cup cilantro, finely chopped

2 tsp. salt

2 Tbsp. olive oil

2 Tbsp. flour

½ cup water

2 cups ricotta cheese

1 cup cottage cheese

2 cups shredded chihuahua cheese, divided

2 eggs

2 Tbsp. finely chopped cilantro

1 tsp. salt

½ tsp. pepper

1 (9-oz.) pkg. noncook lasagne noodles

Makes 12 servings

1 Heat a comal (griddle) to very hot.

2 Roast the whole tomatoes, garlic, and habaneros until charred on all sides.

3 Cut the tops off the tomatoes and habaneros, peel the garlic, and transfer all to a blender. Add the canned tomatoes, cilantro, and salt. Puree until very smooth.

4 Preheat oven to 375 degrees.

5 In a large pot or dutch oven, heat the oil on medium. Add the flour. Stir to make a roux. Remove from heat.

6 Add the puree to the roux. Add water and simmer 12–15 minutes. Set aside to cool.

7 In a large bowl, combine ricotta cheese, cottage cheese, half the chihuahua cheese, eggs, cilantro, salt, and pepper.

**CONTINUED ON NEXT PAGE**

# ASSEMBLING THE LASAGNE

**8** Spread ⅓ of the habanero puree in a deep 9 x 12 baking dish. Cover with a layer of lasagne noodles. Spread half the cheese mixture over the noodles.

**9** Repeat with a second third of sauce, noodles, and the remaining cheese mixture.

**10** Top with remaining habanero sauce and sprinkle with the remaining chihuahua cheese.

**11** Bake for 1 hour. The cheese on top will be golden brown.

**12** Cool for 30 minutes to allow it to set.

Ricardo James

# ESPAGUETI BLANCO

## Spaghetti and Cream | Time: 45 minutes

*My kids love the creamy noodles of this spaghetti. It is similar to an Italian alfredo but is prepared with Mexican flavors and techniques. As commonly done in Mexican cuisine, the pasta is fried before it is boiled.*

1 Tbsp. cooking oil

8 oz. spaghetti, broken in half

¼ white onion

pinch of salt

1 bay leaf

1 allspice berry, whole

3 cups water

### SAUCE

1 Tbsp. cream cheese

¼ cup shredded manchego or chihuahua cheese, divided

1 cup milk

1 chicken bouillon cube (I prefer Knorr brand)

¼ tsp. pepper

Serves 4–6

1 In a large pot, heat oil on medium. Add dry spaghetti noodles along with onion, salt, bay leaf, and allspice berry.

2 Fry until the spaghetti is light brown.

3 Add 3 cups water and boil until spaghetti is al dente and most of the water has evaporated. Remove from heat and set aside. Discard bay leaf. Set the onion and allspice berry aside.

4 Meanwhile, in a blender, puree cream cheese, half of the shredded cheese, milk, bouillon, and pepper until smooth. Add cooked onion and allspice berry. Puree to incorporate.

5 Return the pot to low heat. Add cream sauce to noodles and stir. Simmer until it thickens and coats the noodles.

6 Serve on individual plates and sprinkle with remaining cheese.

**NOTE** *You may also transfer the spaghetti to a casserole dish, top with cheese, and broil until cheese is light brown and bubbling.*

Ricardo James

# SOPA DE ESPAGUETI

## Mexican Spaghetti | Time: 45 minutes

*This is not your familiar Italian spaghetti; it is quite different. The broth is boiled down to almost nothing, the noodles are soft, and the touch of cream adds richness. Remember that this is a primer plato and the portions should be small.*

## NOODLES

1 Tbsp. cooking oil

8 oz. spaghetti, broken in half

¼ medium white onion

pinch of salt

1 bay leaf

1 allspice berry, whole

3 cups water

## SAUCE

3 tomatoes, chopped

¼ medium white onion

1 allspice berry, whole

1 garlic clove

½ cup water

1 Tbsp. butter

½ tsp. granulated chicken bouillon

¼ cup half-and-half

¾ cup shredded manchego or chihuahua cheese

Serves 4–6

1 In a large pot, heat oil on medium. Add dry spaghetti noodles along with onion, salt, bay leaf, and allspice berry. Fry until the spaghetti is light brown.

2 Add 3 cups water and boil until spaghetti is al dente and most of the water has evaporated. Remove from heat and set aside. Discard onion, bay leaf, and berry.

3 Meanwhile, in a small pan, boil the tomatoes, onion, allspice berry, and garlic in water.

4 Transfer to a blender and puree until smooth.

5 Melt butter in small saucepan on medium. Add puree and bouillon and simmer for 5 minutes to thicken.

6 Return the noodles to low heat. Add tomato sauce by pouring through a strainer. Stir. Simmer to heat through.

7 Remove from heat and cool slightly. Add half-and-half. Stir to incorporate. Return to heat and warm to thicken.

8 Serve on individual plates and top with cheese.

**NOTE** *You may also transfer the spaghetti to a casserole dish, top with cheese, and broil until cheese is light brown and bubbling.*

Ricardo James

# ENSALADA DE ELOTE

## Corn Salad | Time: 30 minutes

*Elotes, or corn on the cob, done the Mexican street way are the most wonderful, messy things you'll ever eat. Grilled or boiled elotes are lathered with lime-flavored mayonnaise, rolled in cotija cheese, and then sprinkled with chile powder. My elote salad infuses the same flavors and transforms them into a salad fit for any picnic or barbecue without the mess.*

*Note: For authentic Mexican flavor, grill the corn rather than boiling.*

**6 corn cobs**

**1 medium red onion, diced**

**½ cup cilantro, chopped**

**¾ cup crumbled cotija cheese**

**juice of 3 limes**

**1 tsp. salt**

**1½ cups mayonnaise**

**1–2 tsp. chile powder**

**Serves 10**

1 Grill or boil the cobs for 10 minutes. Remove from heat and cool in a cold water bath.

2 Cut the kernels off the cob into a bowl.

3 Add the diced onion, chopped cilantro, and crumbed cheese and toss.

4 Combine the lime juice, salt, and mayonnaise in a small bowl.

5 Toss the mayonnaise mixture into the corn mixture. Sprinkle with chile powder.

6 Serve warm or cold.

Ricardo James

# ENSALADA DE NOPAL

## Cactus Salad | Time: 35 minutes

*Even though this salad is delicious by itself, and has the name of a salad, it is usually served as a salsa, like you would pico de gallo. You can typically find cactus paddles in a Mexican market. You can find bottled cactus in some supermarkets. If you are lucky enough to find fresh cactus, clean each paddle by cutting off the tough end and then trimming off one-fourth inch all around the edge. Cut off the spines by running a large knife over the cactus paddles several times. Wash thoroughly. This is great on tacos! Note: As the cactus is left to sit, it will weep a sticky goo. I rinse the goo off immediately before adding to the salad, and then I serve quickly.*

**2 cactus paddles**

**4 tomatoes, diced**

**1 small white onion, diced**

**1 serrano chile, minced**

**¼ cup cilantro, chopped**

**salt**

1 Trim and de-spine the cactus paddles. Rinse the cactus and grill or broil on high heat until charred.

2 Dice cactus into 1/2-inch squares.

3 Toss cactus with the tomatoes, onion, chile, and cilantro in a serving bowl.

4 Add salt to taste. Serve immediately.

## Makes approx. 6 cups

Ricardo James

# DRINKS

Bebidas

**M**exico has an abundance of fresh fruits and vegetables. As with food, drinks are presented via traditional presentations, which include aguas, licuados, and jugos. These presentations are easily identified. An agua is a watered-down version of a juice with added sweetener, much like our lemonade. The flavors are limitless. A licuado is much like our smoothie with a milk or yogurt base. A jugo is typically pure juice of one or more ingredients.

Here is a quick list of typical fruits, greens, and vegetables used in aguas that are readily available in most Mexican markets.

Limón (Lime)
Naranja (Orange)
Tangerina (Tangerine)
Nectarina (Nectarine)
Toronja (Grapefruit)
Papaya
Mango
Sandía (Watermelon)
Melón (Cantaloupe)
Melón Verde (Honeydew)
Manzana (Apple)
Pera (Pear)
Kiwi
Carambola (Starfruit)
Pitaya (Dragon Fruit)
Piña (Pineapple)
Coco (Coconut)
Plátano (Banana)
Fresa (Strawberry)
Frambuesa (Raspberry)
Mora (Blackberry)

Arándano (Blueberry)
Uva (Grape)
Durazno (Peach)
Tuna (Prickly Pear)
Flor de Jamaica
  (Hibiscus Flower)
Arroz (Rice)
Cebolla (Onion)
Ajo (Garlic)
Espinaca (Spinach)
Alfalfa
Tomate (Tomato)
Aguacate (Avocado)
Pepino (Cucumber)
Guayaba (Guava)
Maracuyá (Passion Fruit)
Cereza (Cherry)
Tamarindo (Tamarind)
Zanahoria (Carrot)
Apio (Celery)
Betabel (Beet)

I've chosen my favorite aguas to include in this book. These are simple-to-execute recipes that you would find in any Mexican kitchen.

# AGUA DE SANDÍA CON YERBA BUENA

Watermelon-Mint Cooler
Time: 30 minutes (1 hour more with dry ice)

*This delightful agua uses lime for tartness and spearmint leaves for added freshness. Make sure you find a ripe watermelon—green watermelons have a bitter taste. Even though I use a seedless watermelon, I still use a strainer to remove the small yellow seeds. If you can't find a seedless variety, use a traditional melon but use the lowest setting on your blender so as not to break the seeds.*

2 cups sugar

4 cups water

1 small or ½ large
   seedless watermelon

juice of 10 limes

8–10 spearmint leaves

3 quarts cold water

2 lbs. dry ice (optional)


Makes 1 gallon

1 Make a simple syrup by simmering the sugar in 4 cups of water. Heat until the sugar is fully dissolved, about 2 minutes. It does not need to boil. Set aside to cool.

2 Slice the watermelon, cut off the rind, and cut into large cubes. Working in batches, fill your blender with watermelon cubes and cold water. Puree on a medium-low setting to break up the fruit. Be careful not to liquefy the seeds. Pour the watermelon juice through a strainer into a large container. Repeat the process until remaining watermelon has been pureed.

3 Using the blender again, puree the syrup, lime juice, and spearmint leaves on high and pour through the strainer into the watermelon juice.

4 Add any remaining water and stir.

5 Chill and serve on ice.

**OPTIONAL** *One hour before serving, add dry ice and stir occasionally. The dry ice will carbonate the juice and keep it super cold.*

Ricardo James

Drinks

# AGUA DE MELÓN

## Cantaloupe-Ade | Time: 15 minutes

*This exceptional agua is extremely easy, and because cantaloupes are so readily available, you can make this all year round.*

¾ **cup sugar**

2 **cups water**

1 **cantaloupe**

**juice of 4 limes**

2 **Tbsp. honey**

1 **quart ice-cold water**

½ **cup raspberries, frozen, whole (optional)**

**Makes 2 quarts**

1 Make a simple syrup by simmering the sugar in 2 cups of water. Heat until the sugar is fully dissolved, about 2 minutes. It does not need to boil. Set aside to cool.

2 Slice the cantaloupe, remove the seeds, cut off the rind, and cut into large cubes. Fill a blender with the simple syrup, melon cubes, lime juice, honey, and a bit of the cold water. Puree on high until smooth.

3 Pour mixture into a pitcher. Add remaining ice-cold water and serve immediately.

**OPTIONAL** *Garnish with frozen whole raspberries.*

# AGUA DE BETABEL

## Beet-Ade | Time: 30 minutes

*This agua will surprise you—it is extremely healthy and is so good you won't believe it's made of beets. When introducing this agua to friends, don't mention the beets. Let them tell you how good it is first.*

**1 cup sugar**

**2 cups water**

**2 medium beets, cleaned**

**1 tart apple**

**ice**

**juice of 3 limes**

**ice-cold water**

**Makes ½ gallon**

**1** Make a simple syrup by simmering the sugar in 2 cups of water. Heat until the sugar is fully dissolved, about 2 minutes. It does not need to boil. Set aside to cool.

**2** Juice the beets and apple, discarding the leftover pulp.

**3** Fill a half-gallon pitcher halfway full of ice.

**4** Add syrup, beet, apple, and lime juice to ice and top off with water and stir.

**5** Serve cold.

**NOTE** *If you don't have a juicer, you can boil the beets until tender and puree them in a blender with the raw apple. Strain out all the pulp and chill before using.*

Ricardo James

# AGUA DE JAMAICA

## Hibiscus Iced Tea | Time: 45 minutes

*Hibiscus tea is consumed both hot and cold in many parts of the world. However, the crimson-colored, cranberry-tasting agua has been slow to appear in the United States. One more reason we should all make it often.*

**1 cup dried hibiscus flowers**

**4 cups water**

**1 cup sugar**

**ice**

**ice-cold water**

Makes 1 gallon

1 In a saucepan, bring dried flowers and 4 cups of water to a boil. Remove from the heat and steep for 30 minutes.

2 To remove and discard the rehydrated flowers from the tea, place a metal strainer lined with 3 paper towels over a large bowl. Pour the contents of the pan into the strainer, being careful not to break the paper towels.

3 While the tea is still hot, add the sugar and stir until dissolved. (If the tea is cold, reheat and add the sugar.)

4 Fill a gallon pitcher with ice. Add the tea and cold water. Stir. Serve cold.

**NOTE** *Taste for sweetness. Add more sugar if desired.*

Ricardo James

# AGUA DE TAMARINDO

## Tamarind Tea | Time: 45 minutes

*The tamarind tree, originally from Africa, made its way to Mexico in the sixteenth century. It produces an odd-looking fruit consisting of hard-shelled pods that contain the fruit and hard seeds. It makes a refreshing agua.*

½ lb. raw tamarind pods

4 cups water

1 cup sugar

ice

ice-cold water

**Makes 1 gallon**

1 Break the casings off each tamarind pod and discard the hard brittle pieces. Remove the strings inside the pod, leaving only the meaty flesh clinging to the seeds.

2 Put the tamarind and 4 cups water in a saucepan and bring to a boil. Reduce heat and simmer for 30 minutes.

3 Remove from the heat. Add the sugar and dissolve completely.

4 Pour the entire contents into a blender. Blend on the lowest setting as to not break up the seeds. Blend for 2 minutes.

**NOTE** *It will sound like marbles in your blender.*

5 Prepare to strain the tamarind water by placing a metal strainer lined with 3 paper towels over a large bowl. Pour the contents of the blender into the strainer.

6 Chill the tamarind concentrate.

7 When ready to serve, fill a gallon pitcher halfway full of ice. Add concentrate and cold water to the top. Stir and serve cold.

Ricardo James

# AGUA DE MANGO

## Mango-Ade | Time: 10 minutes

*Total bliss! Simple. Pure. Awesomeness. I need not say more.*

**2 large mangoes or
  4 small manila mangoes**

**1 cup sugar**

**2 quarts ice-cold water**

**Makes 2 quarts**

**1** Remove the pit from each mango by standing the mango on end with the stem end up. With a sharp knife, cut from the stem down through the mango, bowing around the pit as you go. Repeat on the other side.

**2** Cut a tic-tac-toe design into the flesh without cutting through the peel. Taking the mango in your hands, press on the peel side, spreading your cuts open. Slice the fruit from the peel.

**3** Remove any mango still attached to the pit.

**4** Place the mango and sugar in a blender. Add water and puree on high until smooth. Repeat if necessary.

**5** Pour into a 2-quart pitcher and top off with water. Stir.

**6** Pour into a glass and consume immediately before someone else does.

Ricardo James

# LIMONADA

## Limeade | Time: 15 minutes

*Limonada is the simplest drink to make. I like mine tart so I add a chopped lime (limón) with the peel intact. Limonada is the most common Mexican drink made at home. In Mexico, lemons (limas) are hard to find, and when you do find them, you'll notice that they are round, yellowish-green, less acidic, and more like a tangelo.*

**juice of 6 limes**

**1 cup sugar**

**1 lime, chopped,
   discard the ends**

**ice-cold water**

**ice**

Makes 2 quarts

1  Put the lime juice, sugar, and chopped lime in a blender with 2 cups of water. Puree on high.

2  Fill a 2-quart pitcher halfway full of ice. Strain the contents of the blender into the pitcher. Top off with water. Stir.

149

# AGUA DE MARACUYÁ

## Passion Fruit–Ade | Time: 20 minutes

*This is my favorite drink by far because I love passion fruit. However, fresh passion fruit is difficult to find where I live. When visiting Central or South America, I order it every chance I get.*

*Note: If you can't find fresh passion fruit, look for bottled concentrate in your local Latin market or online.*

**¾ cup sugar**

**cold water**

**3–4 passion fruit**

**Makes 2 quarts**

1 Make a simple syrup by simmering the sugar in 2 cups of water. Heat until the sugar is fully dissolved, about 2 minutes. It does not need to boil. Set aside to cool.

2 Cut the passion fruit in half. Scrape out the pulp and the seeds into a strainer over a bowl.

3 With a spoon, push the pulp through the strainer, capturing the black seeds. (Rumor has it the seeds may cause stomach problems.)

4 In a 2-quart pitcher, combine pulp, syrup, and enough water to fill the pitcher. Stir until combined.

5 Serve cold.

# AGUA DE PAPAYA

## Papaya-Ade | Time: 25 minutes

*I love fresh papaya with lime, honey, and a little chile powder. Another way to enjoy papaya is in this agua. Where I live, papaya can be expensive. Making a single papaya into an agua stretches its use, and more people can enjoy the unique flavor.*

**1 cup sugar**

**cold water**

**1 large papaya**

**juice of 8 limes**

**2 Tbsp. honey**

**Makes 1 gallon**

1  Make a simple syrup by simmering the sugar in 2 cups of water. Heat until the sugar is fully dissolved, about 2 minutes. It does not need to boil. Set aside to cool.

2  Cut the papaya in half lengthwise.

3  With a spoon, remove all the seeds and discard them.

4  With a knife, cut off the papaya's skin and cut the fruit into large chunks.

5  Place the fruit and the simple syrup in a blender and puree until very smooth. You may have to do this in batches depending on the size of your papaya.

6  Pour puree into a 1-gallon pitcher and add lime juice, honey, and enough water to fill the pitcher.

7  Stir well and keep cold.

**NOTE**  *Papayas come in all sizes. This recipe uses the large variety; however, you might only find small papayas where you live. If so, use two or more for this recipe.*

153

# HORCHATA

## Rice Water | Time: 10 minutes and 3-hour soak time

*The milky, cold drink known as horchata is probably the most commonly known Mexican drink here in the United States. It can be found on many restaurant menus. Horchata did not originate in Mexico; but using rice as the core ingredient is uniquely Mexican. Originally, horchata from Spain was made with barley. Horchata must be served ice cold and should be strained well.*

**1 cup long-grain rice**

**2 quarts water, divided**

**2 tsp. cinnamon**

**1 tsp. vanilla**

**1 can sweetened condensed milk**

**Makes 3 quarts**

1  Place rice in a blender with 2 cups water and the cinnamon. Blend on high for 1 minute to break up the rice.

2  Pour blender contents into a large container and add the remaining water.

3  Let the mixture set at room temperature for 3 hours. Stir occasionally.

4  Puree the rice water in batches until smooth.

5  Strain the mixture through a cheesecloth or strainer lined with paper towels to remove all the solids.

6  Transfer the liquid to a large pitcher.

7  Add vanilla and condensed milk. Stir until incorporated completely.

8  Chill and serve very cold.

Ricardo James

# LICUADO

## Basic Mexican Smoothie | Time: 10 minutes

*Licuados are similar to aguas but have a milk base. You can't go wrong with this recipe. Substitute any fruit or fruit combination. The liquid of a licuado is typically thinner than what you'd expect in a smoothie. Add banana or frozen fruit to make it thicker. A licuado is typically a breakfast drink, whereas a smoothie is more of a dessert.*

**1 cup milk**

**½ cup yogurt**

**¾ cup fresh fruit**

**½ banana**

**1 Tbsp. sugar**

**Makes 1 serving**

1 Put all ingredients in a blender and puree until smooth. Enjoy.

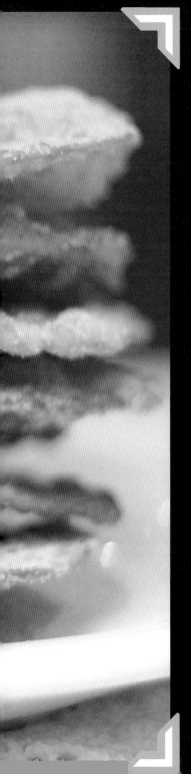

# DESSERTS

## Postres

As I have grown older, I have acquired a sweet tooth that craves the sweet postres of Mexico. Mexican desserts are quite distinct from the desserts we grow up with in the United States: no brownies, chocolate chip cookies, or ice cream. Mexican desserts are unique because their flavors are strong. Cinnamon, caramel, chocolate, and almonds all sound like familiar flavors, but the Mexican twist on each leaves you wondering if they are somehow new to your palate.

# GALLETAS DE BODA

## Mexican Wedding Cookies | Time: 45 minutes

*Each time I visit my Mexican market, I can't resist buying a dozen of these powdered sugar–covered wedding cookies.*

½ cup almonds

1 cup shortening

1 cup sugar

¼ cup milk

1 tsp. vanilla

1 egg

3 cups flour

1 tsp. baking powder

1 Tbsp. cinnamon

½ tsp. ginger

½ tsp. nutmeg

½ tsp. salt

2 cups powdered sugar, for coating

**Makes 5 dozen cookies**

1 Preheat oven to 350 degrees.

2 Using a food processor, chop the almonds into very small pieces. They should resemble course sand. (But processing too long will make a paste.) Set aside.

3 In a large mixing bowl, cream shortening and sugar.

4 Add milk, vanilla, and the egg. Mix well.

5 Add almonds, flour, baking powder, cinnamon, ginger, nutmeg, and salt. Mix well.

6 Roll into 1-inch balls and set on a parchment-lined baking sheet. Slightly flatten each ball.

7 Bake for 7–8 minutes.

8 After the cookies have cooled, roll in powdered sugar until well caked.

# FLAN

Time: 30 minutes, 50-minute cook time,
      3-hour cooling time

*Whether you use teacups, ramekins, or small glass bowls, this creamy flan, with a hint of caramel, is a perfect end to any meal. I prefer to use small glass bowls instead of ramekins because the sides are tapered and they are easier to unmold. This recipe makes six five-ounce portions.*

## CARAMEL

¾ cup sugar

¼ cup water

## CUSTARD

1½ cups milk

1 can sweetened
   condensed milk

1½ cups sugar

1 tsp. vanilla

4 eggs

2 egg yolks

**Makes 6 custards**

1 Prepare 1 quart of very hot water to use as a water bath. Preheat oven to 325 degrees.

## CARAMEL

1 In a small saucepan, heat the sugar and water on medium-high until it comes to a boil.

2 Remove from the heat and allow the sugar to cool slightly.

3 Lower the heat to medium. Return the pan to the heat and let the mixture boil slowly until it turns golden.

4 Begin swirling the pan and continue swirling until you see the color change from gold to caramel.

5 Before the caramel hardens, evenly distribute it into your choice of molds (teacups, ramekins, small glass bowls). Set aside.

**CONTINUED ON NEXT PAGE**

163

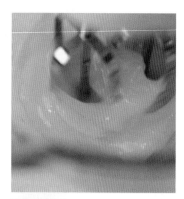

## CUSTARD

**1** In a medium saucepan, bring the milks, sugar, and vanilla to a simmer and remove from the heat before it boils. Set aside to cool.

**2** In a separate bowl, beat the eggs until very smooth.

**3** Temper the eggs by whisking approximately ¼ cup of the hot milk into the eggs.

**4** Slowly whisk the egg mixture back into the milk and pour completed mixture through a fine-mesh strainer to remove any solids.

**5** Pour liquid into the molds, covering the caramel. Place molds into a baking pan.

**6** Place baking pan on the middle rack of the heated oven.

**7** Pour the prepared hot water into the baking pan, surrounding the molds. The water level should match the level of the custard.

**8** Bake for 50 minutes, longer for larger molds. The custard should be slightly firm around the edges.

**9** Cool to room temperature. Cover with plastic wrap and refrigerate until chilled, for at least 3 hours.

**10** To plate, run a small knife around the edge to release the custard from the mold. Invert on a small plate. It should release by itself. Be patient.

**NOTE** *Flavor flan by adding orange zest, lemon zest, or cinnamon with the vanilla. For coconut flan, substitute 1 cup of coconut milk for 1 cup of the regular milk and top with toasted coconut.*

Ricardo James

# FLAN DE CHOCOLATE

Chocolate Flan

Time: 30 minutes, 50-minute cook time,
          3-hour cooling time

## CARAMEL

¾ cup sugar

¼ cup water

## CHOCOLATE CUSTARD

1½ cups milk

1 cup sugar

1 tsp. vanilla

1 Mexican chocolate round
(I recommend Nestle-
Abuelita brand)

4 eggs

2 egg yolks

1 can sweetened
condensed milk

Makes 6 custards

1 Prepare 1 quart of very hot water to use as a water bath. Preheat oven to 325 degrees.

## CARAMEL

1 In a small saucepan, heat the sugar and water on medium high until it comes to a boil.

2 Remove from the heat and allow the sugar to cool slightly.

3 Lower the heat to medium. Return the pan to the heat and let the mixture boil slowly until it turns golden.

4 Begin swirling the pan and continue swirling until you see the color change from gold to caramel.

5 Before the caramel hardens, evenly distribute it into your choice of molds (teacups, ramekins, small glass bowls). Set aside.

CONTINUED ON NEXT PAGE

167

# CHOCOLATE CUSTARD

**1** In a medium saucepan, bring the milk, sugar, and vanilla to a simmer and remove from the heat before it boils.

**2** Heat the chocolate round in the microwave for 1 minute and add to the milk. Whisk to incorporate. Set aside to cool.

**3** In a separate bowl, beat the eggs until very smooth.

**4** Temper the eggs by whisking approximately ¼ cup of the hot milk into the eggs.

**5** Slowly whisk the egg mixture back into the milk and pour completed mixture through a fine-mesh strainer to remove any solids.

**6** Pour liquid into the molds, covering the caramel. Place molds into a baking pan.

**7** Place baking pan on the middle rack of the heated oven.

**8** Pour the prepared hot water into the baking pan, surrounding the molds. The water level should match the level of the custard.

**9** Bake for 50 minutes, longer for larger molds. The custard should be slightly firm around the edges.

**10** Cool to room temperature. Cover with plastic wrap and refrigerate until chilled.

**11** To plate, run a small knife around the edge to release the custard from the mold. Invert on a small plate. It should release by itself. Be patient.

Ricardo James

# CHOCOLATE

## Hot Chocolate

## Time: 15 minutes

*Traditional Mexican chocolate is thick, rich, and grainy. Mexicans use a hand mill, or molino, to break up the small chunks of sugar inherent in the Mexican chocolate rounds. When warming the hot chocolate, use a molino in your pot, rubbing the handle back and forth between your hands. The spinning action causes the hot chocolate to froth, allowing the bands around the molino to break up the sugar.*

**4 cups half-and-half**

**1 Mexican chocolate round (I recommend the Nestle-Abuelita brand)**

**Makes 1 quart**

1 Simmer half-and-half in large saucepan. Do not boil. Remove from heat.

2 Melt the chocolate round in the microwave and add to half-and-half. Stir.

Ricardo James

# PLÁTANOS FRITOS

Fried Bananas | Time: 30 minutes

⅔ cup sour cream

juice of 1 orange

¼ cup sugar

1 large plantain

½ cup cooking oil


**Makes 4 servings**

1  Combine sour cream, orange juice, and sugar in a small bowl. Refrigerate until serving.

2  Slice the plantain on a diagonal to make large ovals.

3  Heat oil in a large frying pan.

4  Fry plantains in batches of 7–8 until golden brown. Drain on paper towels.

5  Plate by aligning several plantain chips in a small bowl. Drizzle with orange cream.

173

# BUÑUELOS

Cinnamon Crisps

Time: 25 minutes, 3- to 5-hour drying time,
     30-minute cook time

*These holiday treats can be purchased on the streets. They can be quite large, even larger than a dinner plate. You can drizzle yours with caramel, chocolate, strawberry syrup, or honey, but this recipe will help you make small buñuelos with cinnamon-sugar. Learning to make them yourself doesn't limit this goodie to just the holidays.*

¾ cup milk

4 Tbsp. butter

1 tsp. vanilla

2 eggs

3 cups flour, plus more

1 tsp. cinnamon

2 tsp. baking powder

1 tsp. salt

vegetable oil for frying

## CINNAMON-SUGAR COATING

2 tsp. cinnamon

2 cups sugar

Makes 20 buñuelos

1  In a small saucepan heat the milk, butter, and vanilla to a simmer. Do not boil. Remove from heat.

2  Beat the eggs in a small bowl. To temper the eggs, pour a little of the hot mixture into the eggs while whisking. Pour the egg mixture back into the milk and whisk vigorously to combine. Set aside to cool for 10 minutes.

3  Meanwhile, put the flour, cinnamon, baking powder, and salt in a food processor and pulse to combine.

4  While running the food processor, slowly add the warm liquid mixture and process for 2 minutes. The dough should be very soft and pliable.

NOTE  *If your food processor came with a knead feature, you can now justify your purchase.*

5  Form the dough into 20 small balls.

CONTINUED ON NEXT PAGE

**6** Using a rolling pin and a little flour, roll the balls into thin, tortilla-like shapes.

**7** Let them dry for several hours or overnight, flipping to dry evenly. This removes the extra moisture before frying.

**8** In a large baking pan, combine cinnamon and sugar. Set aside to use during frying.

**9** Using a large frying pan, warm one inch of oil to medium heat.

**10** Slide a buñuelo under the surface of the oil. It will immediately begin to bubble and fry.

**11** Using large tongs or a spatula, keep the buñuelo immersed in the oil.

**NOTE** *It is important not to let the buñuelo float because large bubbles will fill with steam, deforming your buñuelo and risking an oil explosion.*

**12** The buñuelo will turn golden brown on the bottom side in 5–8 seconds. Using your tongs, carefully turn it over and fry for an additional 3–5 seconds.

**13** Remove the buñuelo from the oil, allowing extra oil to drain.

**14** While warm, coat the buñuelo with the cinnamon-sugar mixture.

**15** Repeat steps for all buñuelos. Stand them in a large container lined with paper towels to cool.

# COOKING MEASUREMENT EQUIVALENTS

| Cups | Tablespoons | Fluid Ounces |
|---|---|---|
| ⅛ cup | 2 Tbsp. | 1 fl. oz. |
| ¼ cup | 4 Tbsp. | 2 fl. oz. |
| ⅓ cup | 5 Tbsp. + 1 tsp. | |
| ½ cup | 8 Tbsp. | 4 fl. oz. |
| ⅔ cup | 10 Tbsp. + 2 tsp. | |
| ¾ cup | 12 Tbsp. | 6 fl. oz. |
| 1 cup | 16 Tbsp. | 8 fl. oz. |

| Cups | Fluid Ounces | Pints/Quarts/Gallons |
|---|---|---|
| 1 cup | 8 fl. oz. | ½ pint |
| 2 cups | 16 fl. oz. | 1 pint = ½ quart |
| 3 cups | 24 fl. oz. | 1½ pints |
| 4 cups | 32 fl. oz. | 2 pints = 1 quart |
| 8 cups | 64 fl. oz. | 2 quarts = ½ gallon |
| 16 cups | 128 fl. oz. | 4 quarts = 1 gallon |

## Other Helpful Equivalents

| | |
|---|---|
| 1 Tbsp. | 3 tsp. |
| 8 oz. | ½ lb. |
| 16 oz. | 1 lb. |

# METRIC MEASUREMENT EQUIVALENTS

## Approximate Weight Equivalents

| Ounces | Pounds | Grams |
|--------|--------|-------|
| 4 oz. | ¼ lb. | 113 g |
| 5 oz. | | 142 g |
| 6 oz. | | 170 g |
| 8 oz. | ½ lb. | 227 g |
| 9 oz. | | 255 g |
| 12 oz. | ¾ lb. | 340 g |
| 16 oz. | 1 lb. | 454 g |

## Approximate Volume Equivalents

| Cups | US Fluid Ounces | Milliliters |
|------|-----------------|-------------|
| ⅛ cup | 1 fl. oz. | 30 ml |
| ¼ cup | 2 fl. oz. | 59 ml |
| ½ cup | 4 fl. oz. | 118 ml |
| ¾ cup | 6 fl. oz. | 177 ml |
| 1 cup | 8 fl. oz. | 237 ml |

## Other Helpful Equivalents

| | |
|---|---|
| ½ tsp. | 2½ ml |
| 1 tsp. | 5 ml |
| 1 Tbsp. | 15 ml |

# INDEX

# ABOUT THE AUTHOR

RICHARD M. JAMES grew up in the kitchen. He learned the art of cooking by trial and error. The errors ended up in the garbage, but the trials got better and better. At age nineteen he traveled to Mexico to serve as a missionary among the people, in their homes and in their kitchens. Richard is the father of five and now resides in Utah. He occasionally, with his family, visits Mexico to gather more traditional culinary ideas and techniques.